We Are All Born Mediums

A Do It Yourself Guide That Insists On the Easy Development of Mediumship

By
Paul and Deborah Rees

www.capallbann.co.uk

We Are All Born Mediums

©Copyright 2012 Paul & Deborah Rees

ISBN 1861633394
ISBN 13 9781861633392

ALL RIGHTS RESERVED

Paul & Deborah Rees have asserted their right under the Copyright Designs and Patents Act of 1988 to be identified as the authors of this work
No part of this publication may be reproduced, stored in a retrieval system or transmitted in any form or by any means, electronic, mechanical, photocopying, scanning, recording or otherwise without the prior written permission of the author and the publisher.

Cover design by HR Print and Design Ltd

Published by:

        Capall Bann Publishing
        Auton Farm
        Milverton
        Somerset
        TA4 1NE

Contents

Introduction	1
Chapter 1 If I Can Do It, So Can You!	3
Chapter 2 Mediumistic Versus Psychic	6
Chapter 3 Welcome to Spiritual Hollywood	14
Chapter 4 The Beginner: Keeping It Easy	25
Chapter 5 My Self-Analysis	36
Chapter 6 Your Mediumship: The Starting Block, Responsibility, and Your Product	38
Chapter 7 My Quarterly Self-Assessment	44
Chapter 8 My Analogy; Your Understanding!	48
Chapter 9 You Are the Technician	52
Chapter 10 My Awakening	58
Chapter 11 How to Deal with Nerves in Your Work	68
Chapter 12 The Father Who Once Was	71
Chapter 13 Ghosts	76
Chapter 14 Soul Groups	84
Chapter 15 Do Animals Have a Spirit?	92
Chapter 16 Stress-Free Mediumship: The Format	98
Chapter 17 My Format	103
Chapter 18 Conducting Professional One to One Readings	109
Chapter 19 My One to One Readings	114
Chapter 20 Spirit and Clarity in the English Language	123
Chapter 21 Maintaining the Quality of Your Message	126
Chapter 22 Life's Upside Down, You Can't Think - Off to Work You Go!	130
Chapter 23 Practice, Practice, Practice!	133
Chapter 24 The Secret to a Good Demonstration	137
Chapter 25 My Demonstrations	144
Chapter 26 The Answer is Never NO: Just Look Again	149
Chapter 27 Ego Within Your Work	152
Chapter 28 Why Do We Need to Brag?	157

Chapter 29	Positive Affirmations Are Your Best Friend	160
Chapter 30	My Positive Affirmations	165
Chapter 31	What Is A Guide?	166
Chapter 32	How I Got To Know My Guides	172
Chapter 33	Me and My Guides	183
Chapter 34	Using Symbols Within Mediumship	188
Chapter 35	Me and My Symbols	192
Chapter 36	Meditation and Mediumship	194
Chapter 37	Sensitivity and Mediumship	198
Chapter 38	Teacher Mediums: The Blind Teaching the Blind	201
Chapter 39	The (Sometimes Crazy) Ambassadors of Mediumship	205
Chapter 40	Do We Need Protection?	207
Chapter 41	Global Spiritualism and the Phrase Psychic/Medium	211
Chapter 42	My Goals	216
Chapter 43	Recommended Reading	219

Introduction

All people are special and all moments are golden. There is no person and there is no time, one more special than the other. Many people choose to believe that God communicates in special ways and only with special people. This removes the mass of the people from responsibility for hearing my message, much less receiving it, and allows them to take someone else's word for everything.
Neale Donald Walsh b.1943

For too long the words mediumship, sensitive and psychic have been reserved for those individuals deemed "gifted," or to those with an extra sensitive sixth sense. In this book, professional teacher-mediums Paul and Deborah Rees will prove to you how this complete misconception has been taught to millions globally for approximately 140 years. We will also expose the unspoken working secrets that give favoured international mediums the edge of expertise - secrets they refuse to share for fear of being superseded.

Paul and Deborah, founders of the Accolade Academy of psychic and mediumistic studies, have spent many years travelling the world and revamping the introduction of this aged practice for students of Accolade's development courses. In the process, they have created a method of study that remolds perceptions of and approaches to mediumship, improving intuition and ease of use for thousands of individuals globally. Proven in Accolade Academy classes many times over, this method ensures that this intuitive ability can no longer be reserved for the chosen few. Regardless of your experience - novice, hobbyist or working professional medium - this book is your perfect handbook, journal and future all in one.

Here, Paul and Debs have put together a step-by-step guide with a very real, no-nonsense approach to your intuitive spiritual development. Combining easy to understand strategies for getting started with personal worksheets and new concepts in learning, this book is certain to improve your professional one to one readings and theatre demonstrations overnight. No mysticism, no vague explanations and no more guesswork. You can do this! You can make contact to loved ones passed a proven reality for your colleagues and your clients!

We are all born mediums!

Chapter 1

If I Can Do It, So Can You!

Hide not your talents, they for use were made. What's a sundial in the shade?

Benjamin Franklin

Yes, it's true. If I can make a living with my mediumship, then so can you. How have Debs and I made a successful career for ourselves? Good old-fashioned hard work, and the odd sacrifice here and there.

Did I wait for Spirit to choose my path for me? I would say no. I made a conscience choice; I needed a job and that was it. Although some might argue that point with me, as many a working spiritualist or medium insist that divine interventions from spirit got me where I am in my working career. There is an old claim that mediums are born not made, and while I agree that there have been some fantastic synchronicities in my career (and synchronicity is a leader in success),

I must also say that free will is equally important. If I choose to work fourteen-hour days to make my career a success, then that's my choice, not an intervention of spirit. Some would argue here as well; Debs and I have been told by many mediums, "You must rest. You must have time for yourselves." As if spirit (who they say is in charge) would work one into an early grave! Wouldn't it be in spirit's best interest to look after workers?

Accolade's services have reached many parts of the USA, Canada, and Europe with repeat tours booked for the west and east coasts of the US. If I had a penny for each time someone asked how we've managed to make it this far, I would be a rich man. But why is our success such a big deal? I am hugely grateful for my life and thank the universe every day, but I also think that professional success and longevity are fairly simple objectives. They are the result of manifesting our thoughts; you know the old saying, we are what we think.

As I said, Debs and I have experienced a huge amount of synchronicity and luck over the last eight years, but we have also made the most of every opportunity, no matter how small, never taking our eye off the ball. You have to treat your mediumship as a constant, moving product, never standing still, never relaxing into a place of contentment. Do you think Richard Branson was happy just selling one Virgin product? Of course not!

That raises another issue: some people don't agree with using the word "product" to describe our services, but that's exactly what we are - a product offering a service for payment. It sounds harsh, does it not? But it is still very true. To make a success of this career, you must first get to know what it is you are selling. Ask yourself - what is it you are offering? If you answer "Spirit" then think again. What you are really doing is dealing in clients' feelings and emotions, and the bottom line is, the selling and dealing of emotions is a very competitive business. Mediums are very low on the food chain of needs, coming way after the electric, gas, and water bills. We fall somewhere in the bracket of spare cash when the client has it, a treat maybe, or even a luxury. But don't let that put you off, as there is still plenty of work to go round and lots of customers out there. You just have to work hard and offer a service that is better than the last medium your client saw. Remember, your job is to sell yourself - you are the product. You must identify what makes you different from any other medium or healer. Everyday, envision your services being better. If you do not, you will blend in with the rest and your career will either be short-lived or never reach a place that can sustain a decent standard of living.

Another helpful question to ask yourself is - would you go to yourself as a medium. Swallow your pride and have a good look. I had to, and still do so daily. And don't just look inside, as how you present yourself is also important. The quality of your mediumship alone will not be enough. Gone are the days of the smelly medium in the damp home with spiders and cobwebs!

What I have learned these last eight years with Accolade, with all the travelling and teaching and demonstrations, is that people are people no matter where you are in the world. Above all else, they want a first class service and value for their money. As long as you are prepared to work hard on both your mediumship and yourself, as long as you are willing to see where you need improvement, and as long as you are able to understand that what you consider good enough will always be temporary, then you will be able to offer something special, and that will make you a successful medium. Go on, go for it! We did!

Chapter 2

Mediumistic Versus Psychic

Free will means that you have the choice to connect to spirit...or not.

Wayne Dyer b.1940

Perhaps it would be best to begin by exploring some basic terminology. Most mediums are of the view that a medium can be psychic but a psychic cannot be a medium. This is a subject that is debated almost daily all over the world, yet very few offer any clear solutions. When they do, everyone involved has their own ideas as to who is right and who is wrong. In order to explain my view on the subject, let's start by looking at the meaning of each word.

According to the Farflex online dictionary, Mediumistic is an adjective describing anything "of or relating to a spiritual medium."

The word Medium, again according to Farflex, is a "person supposedly used as a spiritual intermediary between the dead and the living."

And the word Psychic, this time according to Wikipedia.org, refers to "a person who professes an ability to perceive information hidden from the normal senses through extrasensory perception (ESP), or who is said by others to have such abilities. The word 'psychic' is also used to describe theatrical performers, such as stage magicians, who use techniques such as prestidigitation, cold reading, and hot reading to produce the appearance of such abilities."

Looking at these three words, we can see how easy it would be to manipulate the definitions in order to make them fit a particular view. Our next step, then, is to gain a greater understanding of each word and its relevance to our conversation. Since "mediumistic" is a derivative, we'll start with its root word, "medium."

In our profession, medium is a fairly simple word, used to describe a person who can communicate with the dead and relay information from the dead to a person or persons on the earthly plane, but not the other way round.

A little more complicated, psychic is the word that causes the most debate. As noted, the online definition is quite open: "a person who professes an ability to perceive information hidden from the normal senses through extrasensory perception (ESP)." Wow, you might think, psychics have it pretty good. After all, "information" can pertain to, or define, any number of thoughts and ideas. It can reference something as specific as a client's bank information, or as broad as the details of your client's family in spirit. Perhaps it could even be both. If that's the case, I'm changing my title from psychic medium to just psychic, as that would allow more freedom in defining my services than any I could offer.

Unfortunately, the distinction between the two words is somewhat vague. I've seen many good psychics who, while working with individual clients or large audiences, deliver both great evidence relating to a recipient's life, and also great spiritual evidence of loved ones passed. Agreed, the spiritual evidence of loved ones in spirit may not carry the same level of detail that some mediums deliver, but nevertheless, it's still good quality. We have a woman named Psychic Sally here in the UK, for instance, who is a great evidential psychic. Or is she a medium? This is where things get confusing, and this is where I must ask - what are the underlying reasons for the stigma behind using the term medium versus psychic? Why do many established working mediums look down on working psychics as if they are the poor relations of our movement?

For simplicity, in my next argument, I am going to place all mediums, psychics, and sensitive's under one label, called the "worker."

Let's start with a typical example: a worker is giving evidence of a loved one passed and the contact from spirit is accepted by the recipient/client as being correct. The worker then gives the recipient guidance or a message regarding a certain issue in the recipient's life as part of the communication. This is often information which the recipient claims only the spirit contact could have known. What title should we give that worker? Would you say he or she is a medium or a psychic? Many would suggest that mediums do not give messages or any kind of guidance from spirit contacts regarding a recipient's life matters. Hard core, loyal spiritual mediums would suggest that all messages given within any communication would be considered working on a psychic level. I disagree.

For me, the suggestion that all messages or guidance are gained by reading the recipient psychically just does not make practical sense. What if my dad came to me from spirit via a medium and wanted to give me a message of support during a difficult time in my life? Should that working medium say to him, "Sorry mate, no can do. I don't deliver messages within my communications, as that would make me a psychic"? Would my dad step back and refuse to give a message to a medium, thinking he should wait for a psychic to cross my path to deliver the message for him? The real question here regards the message: is the message mediumistic or psychic? And this is where we must define our own beliefs. I personally feel that if a message is delivered from a loved one passed via the worker, whether regarding the recipient's life or some other subject, it must be considered mediumistic, as the loved one is the contact relaying the message to the worker.

Now let us consider another issue. What if my dad did not validate himself, but the same message was given. Would that be considered a psychic rather than a mediumistic message? This is the root of the confusion between psychic and mediumistic.

Let's go back and look at this from the opposite prospective. Let's say a psychic delivered the message. It's said that a psychic cannot link with spirit, that any information comes directly from the reading of the client's soul, aura, mind, energy, higher self, and/or spiritual being. Others say that a psychic links with the recipient's spirit guide whilst reading. Debs will discuss spirit guides more fully in a later chapter. For now, let me just say that this is another head-scratcher for me, as talking to a client's guides, if possible, must by definition mean the psychic is linking to spirit. It is as if the realms of mediumship or the land of spirit have been barred from all workers titled "psychic."

Let's take another example. A psychic gives evidence of a relative in spirit (regardless of the quantity of evidence) who then gets validated and accepted by the recipient. But say they had never actually met in real life but that the recipient knew of the relative by name only. Where, then, is that information coming from? I would say from all of the places listed above. But, you may ask, how can that be? My answer is simple. If claimed psychic evidence comes from actual events in a client's life, then it must follow that all mediums are psychic and all psychics are mediums. Not according to most proponents of the spiritual movement, of course, but nonetheless I believe that is the evidence. Looking to the dictionary explanations above, in fact, it would appear that a psychic explanation has more strength behind it than would a mediumistic one, at least in a technical sense.

Returning to the dictionary definition of psychic. This states that a psychic can only "cold read" or "hot read." In this case, the psychics I know do themselves an injustice. Let me explain. A hot reading is one in which the psychic secretly researches the client's information prior to the actual reading. A cold read is where the Psychic doesn't ask for or have any information before hand. Rather he or she claims to read the recipient's mind, picking up on body language, etc. Say the psychic demonstrates in a theatre and chooses a recipient from the audience. The chosen individual is sitting in the back row where it is nearly impossible for the psychic to see them, let alone read their body language. If all of the evidence given proves correct, then one must ask - from where is the psychic obtaining his or her evidence? If this particular situation eliminates the psychic's ability to visually read a person in the audience, and I believe it does, then in my opinion the answer must be that the information comes from spirit.

We can go further with this one. What if the person being read can't be seen at all? Suppose he or she is in another room and the psychic has no idea of gender, age, or background. Just to be sure, let's say the recipient's voice is also disguised or changed, and the psychic has not made any precious audible contact with the client in any way. Yet, the psychic is still able to give evidence that is accurate and personal to the client. Again, from where is the psychic obtaining evidence? Most spiritualists and working mediums claim that a psychic must have, at the very least, some visual, audible or energetic exchange with a client in order to psychically read that person. Again, I believe the evidence, in this case, must come from spirit.

Some of Accolade's courses use a psychic exercise called Numbers and Partners that supports my theory that all evidence comes from one place. Let me explain. In the exercise, numbers are written on several small pieces of paper, which are then discreetly distributed. If there are sixteen students, each gets a number from one to eight, with all numbers being duplicated once. In this way, each student will have a number that corresponds with another student's. No student has any knowledge about who they are partnered with and no student handles or sees any number other than his/her own. This eliminates any possibility of a student being able to psychically read their numbered partner by way of the spirit, soul, aura, mind, or energy by contact (vocal or visual) with a spiritual being. We can even split hairs and include the "higher self" or "higher source" here, allowing that the student still has the opportunity to read their partnered student's higher self/source. I say this because it could be claimed by some (not me) that a psychic connection is still available by way of the familiarity of identical numbers.

Let me digress a bit here. For me, the term "higher self or higher source" is a very grey area, as it's a subject even less understood than the medium/psychic debate I present here. I mean, if we can get detailed evidence of loved ones passed from our "higher self or higher source" then what's the point in using the words "spirit" or "spirit world"? Theoretically, we would all be able to tap into to a universal connection of what once was, accessing what is essentially an open door in the universe that allows us to reach loved ones passed. In some vague way it's easier for me to work with the words "universal connection," as that phrase is far more practical and simplistic (than having to imagine a spirit world). Morally speaking, would using "universal connection" instead of "spirit world" be okay for me? Possibly, as I feel these words are more easily understood and accepted in everyday language. This, I would say, is mostly due to the confidence we have acquired this last decade through a growing awareness of the universal, individual, positive law of attraction. Somehow I don't think this growth would have been possible if those preaching positive thoughts used words or labels like "spirit world" instead of "law of attraction." For me, if a change of one word or title allows a greater acceptance and use of mediumship globally, then I say go for it.

Okay, back to Numbers and Partners. After receiving their numbers, students are instructed to go home and write down any evidence that comes through on their partner. They've already been advised that it is wise not to have a particular class member in mind prior to starting their homework, the concern being that personal, visual opinions of fellow students could supersede true evidence. Now here's the thing, students are given the freedom to write whatever evidence comes whilst remaining mindful that this is a "psychic" exercise. Remember, they have no idea who they are partnered with. Rather, they are to write a psychic reading based solely on what they feel from the number. The next day, they read their homework to the class. What happens is that students firstly set their mind and thoughts to psychic mode; the moment the mind focuses on the homework exercise, students unknowingly and naturally open their feelings and thoughts to becoming receptive to the thoughts and feelings from spirit.

In most cases the assignments shared in class the next day show clear, accurate evidence given from spirit through messages that correspond to their partners' loved ones passed. Yes, you read correct. And if I'm not mistaken our hard-core spiritual mediums would call such actual evidence of a beloved from spirit a mediumistic, not psychic, link. Is it possible to reach out to the psychic higher self/source of the partnered student and get that kind of spiritual evidence? Some might say yes, if that contact was still in the memory of the student, but on many occasions the spiritual contact has been validated by the student, but did not have any associating role/part in the students living life.

Most mediums carry the view that a medium can be psychic but a psychic cannot be a medium, but in my opinion we are all mediumistic. Some workers choose to work harder than others when presenting evidence, and aim to get more detail for their client, always pushing for the perfect validation. Other workers convince themselves they only have a so- called psychic ability, and so concentrate on the message, steering clear of evidence that really matters. Why, I can't say. I don't understand any reasoning behind not reaching for all available evidence. The hard part is done, as the worker is already in the mindset for a particular job and receiving/giving evidence of someone from spirit is right there for the taking. Indeed, giving actual confirmation that our loved ones are there for us not only does good, it also strengthens the message portion of the communication.

Some things in life will never be resolved or understood; maybe we are looking too hard and searching for complications that do not exist. I often find it's the least educated that have the most to say on subjects they claim to own, and I'm afraid this one, Medium Versus Psychic, is in the premier league of arbitration. These views are simply my own, shared in order to help you develop an informed opinion. I have spent may hours listening to experienced individuals from all over the world debate this subject and I always end up back in the same place, wondering why something so naturally easy has to be so naturally difficult to understand in the eyes of many.

I decided long ago to keep my psychic mediumship as simple as I can. I told myself that if I made this field my living then it would be a living that others could understand. For me, ALL evidence, regardless of content, comes from one place: SPIRIT.

Now you must decide the issue for yourself!

Chapter 3
Welcome to Spiritual Hollywood

Hollywood grew to be the most flourishing factory of popular mythology since the Greeks.

Alistair Cooke

"Welcome to spiritual Hollywood!" Those were my thoughts uring the first few months of working as a medium. When first introduced to the land of mediumship and the realms of spiritualism, I truly felt like I was surrounded by attention seeking children rather than grown adults. It seemed like every self-acclaimed medium I met wanted nothing more than to lord his or her experience over the next medium in the firing line. Sometimes this was a case of the more practiced workers trying to impress newcomers (like me), but generally, this happened among friends, who tried to best one another behind each other's backs like sly foxes pinching someone else's favourite foods. When I began, I had very little experience, and boy did some of the local Welsh mediums make the most of that.

Mediumship is a subject within many subjects, because it is used for in so many spiritual and/or intuitive disciplines, from spiritual healing, trance healing, and paranormal investigations, to spiritual trance where the contact from spirit speaks through a medium using their (the spirit's) own voice.

These are just a few, and for a medium, it can feel like being overshadowed, though in a good way. Mediumship is like a story that has no beginning and no end. A field that, if it is to be accepted professionally, must fight its already undeserved mystic reputation globally, whilst also trying to sieve out the exploitations of our seasoned spiritual mediums' makebelieve mystic happenings.

My very first visit to a local spiritualist church was on a Thursday evening. It was an open circle night, where they are open to the public. Everyone sat in a circle as we were guided in meditation by a senior church leader. After meditation each person proceeded to take turns passing on messages from a loved one in spirit to someone sitting in the circle. Wow, I thought, this can't be all that difficult. All I needed to do was relay my feelings and thoughts. After all, if that was something so difficult to do that one would have to be so angelic as to hover, then no one would have even been there. They would have been off earning their millions elsewhere.

About three months prior to that night, I had gone to see the local "fortune teller," at least that's what my mother called her after her yearly visits. We always gathered round and read my mother's notes on arriving home, sitting in astonishment at the fortune teller's accuracy. How did she know? If I only knew then what I do now.

To this day I have mixed emotions as to why I went to see her, why I felt the need to see her. Why not just go to a shrink? After all, is that not the thing to do when you feel you are losing your mind? Who knows, maybe it was my calling in some way, as it seemed to be a natural something that I felt I needed to experience. Anyhow, to cut a long story short - I paid the "fortune teller" a visit and boy was I in for a surprise.

I had never met this lady before in my life and yet she knew me so well. I was a little embarrassed to say the least: as she started to read me I was overwhelmed by emotion, the same feeling you get when watching a sad movie that has a happy ending. It was a good feeling and I remember thinking, "Why am I crying? Where did these emotions come from? I could not work it out; it was as if my sensitivity levels went from zero to overdrive in a second flat, as she unfolded my life and all my darkest secrets. Then she claimed my grandmother was there from spirit. I was engulfed in waves of emotion again and again. In a way, I suppose it felt like a reunion with someone I loved and had not seen for a lifetime, but without physically experiencing their presence. "Man up," I kept repeating to myself, shouting it as loud as I could in my mind. But it made no difference. It was as if I wasn't in charge of my own, overwhelming tears. That depth of an emotion was something I had never felt before. As she handed me a tissue, the fortune teller said, "You have a natural ability to link with spirit yourself. You need to find a development circle."

After forty-five minutes of tears and emotions you would think I would have been exhausted, but no I felt energised as if I had just left a huge celebration of gratitude in my name. I felt like I could go out and run a marathon, it was that same kind of awakened energy I used to have as a child on Christmas morning

When I left, I was on a mission, wondering what she meant by "a natural ability," and where I could find a so-called spiritualist church. I spent the next few weeks hunting the streets of Wales looking for what I thought would be a fantastic, historically preserved building. My first surprise was to realize that was not the case. The spiritualist religion has to be one of the least funded religions in the UK and the physical churches are generally leftover fabricated buildings erected during the second World War. Anyhow, I found a church locally and that is where it all started - the weekly, open development circle.

What the notice-board should have said was, "Weekly ego workout every Thursday night."

Still, after that first night I was hooked. It was so easy. All I did was relay each feeling and thought to whomever I thought I needed to say it to. "What's the fuss," I wondered. "Why all the mysticism, and talk of opening and closing one's self?" That was what they called it when they wanted you to visualise shutting down the spiritual connection between yourself and the spirit world. Mmmmmm, all a little strange, but I was new, and decided to go with it. After the third week, the what seemed like a hundred-year-old senior leader decided I was too open. Now this is a strange one. He claimed to think I was too advanced with my ability to link to spirit and that I did not have enough experience to manage my newly adopted mediumship. Then he said he was afraid spirit was taking advantage of me, and strongly advised I see him after the circle finished.

There were five of us left at the end of the evening; Mr. Senior Leader (I don't remember his name), three of his closest helpers, and me. They stood me in the middle of the room and switched the lights out. Then the four of them started humming loudly, claiming this would help control the oversized link between myself and the spirit world, the spirit world being the spiritualist church's word used for a place they feel our loved ones go once they pass over. At that moment, my idea of going to a shrink (before the fortune teller) felt like it would have been the better option. Should I embarrass them and walk out? They were so wrapped up in what they were doing, and though I did not want to hurt their feelings, I was sceptical. Was this really for my benefit, or theirs, I wondered. What's the point, and what the hell does it mean "too open." It was like a comedy show, I mean what's next, being beamed up like in *Star Trek*? I was thirty-three years of age, and had never felt the need to open or close my being. I mean, I was just me.

I'm not sure what it was they were trying to achieve, but truthfully I felt no different that night than I have any other night of my life.That was my first taste of spiritualism, or at least the side that is led by the ego. What I learned that night was that even mediumship has its quircks, who want only to take advantage of another's naivety. That's a shame, as I truly love spiritualism and will always do the most I can to support and help finance the churches in the UK and all over the world. Maybe as time passes we can expose this kind of unnerving practice, as regaining the confidence of the public is a must for this struggling religion.

After that night, I spent the next couple of weeks going to different development circles around town, each with its own style and beliefs. Although they varied considerably, all seemed to share a list of suffocating rules that were made up as people saw fit. Some were so crazy! For instance, listening to some of the mediums I came into contact with then, one would believe it was nearly impossible to function as a medium for fear of being overpowered by some dark entity. This was due to the insistence, as I've already discussed, that you should pray for Protection, or at the least complete some kind of power ritual. Surely mediumship is not meant to be that stressful. After all, this ability is one of the most natural feelings I have ever worked with, as natural as taking a breath in and releasing breath out. Should I ask for protection from negative energies whilst breathing due to the fear of sucking in something dangerous? "Please god, protect me whilst I breath!" What do you think?

I have no doubt there could be a million reactions to my opinion on this, just like the other million suffocating rules I endured. Although I value free will and although a variety of opinions are vital for growth, I found the first few months within this movement a little childish to say the least. Grown adults fighting for leadership just like they would in war games on the school playground. This may sound a little harsh, but these untrained volunteers who claim to carry all the love and light this world can deliver gave very little thought to my emotions or what I thought was good for me.

The aim of this book is not to write about all the negative events that I have experienced. Fortunately, these are in the minority. What I hope to do by recounting these events is prevent you from going through some of the same struggles. Sadly, most of my difficulties in the early development of my spiritual mediumship were the result of choosing the wrong people to consult for assistance. My advice to you is always check the background of the person (or people) you are being mentored by. Never stick to one mentor/teacher, as experiencing a wide array of methods and opinions is better than only one. If a mentor wants you to be taught by him/her exclusively, then get out of there as this is usually a move to control your mediumship and/or your money. Any teachers worth their salt will want you to experience as much as you can from as many as you can. They will also leave it to you to decide what is good or bad advice. You see, mediumship is an area of self-development, and a discipline that has to come from your own self-trust. That trust will also come from your strength in making choices - that will benefit not just you but others.

I wasted my senior school years, spending much of my time vandalising any part of the campus I could get away with vandalising and smoking cigarettes in order to be a part of the toughest gang. As a result, I left school having accomplished very little, whilst carrying the additional inconvenience of being dyslexic. There weren't many choices available as far as employment went. My dad's words of encouragement were, "I bet you will never find work." That was his idea of instilling confidence. Yet coming from a place where his hope was I would prove him wrong.

My primary reason for becoming a working medium was that I needed a job. I had shifted through a series of the usual labour-intense jobs before finding work in an upholstery factory. That was the next decade and half of my life. That's also when my life's education really started. Upholstery is an industry known for its keep-up-or-loose-out attitude. There were constant battles between shopfloor and main board directors over wages and working conditions. I stuck to it, though, eventually becoming part of a national negotiating team that represented a workforce of two and a half thousand employees. It was during these years that I learnt so much about peoples' needs and running a business. Those days proved to be invaluable to the birth of Accolade Academy.

Synchronicity is a wonderful tool; one so perfect that self-recognition and trust in your life will always reward you with a perfect flow. This realisation came to me the moment my upholstery/negotiating career came to an end. I mean, who would have thought Paul Rees would become a medium? Not many, that's for sure.

Going to the fortune teller, finding a spiritualist church, and attending the many local development circles gave me the few weeks training I would get under my belt before being offered a full time position in a local store. My job was to be giving one to one readings in a tiny spare room on the top floor of the building. I shared that room with stacked lengths of timber that were used for the picture-framing part of the shop's services to the public It all happened so fast. I would say it was about eight weeks, going from the upholstery business, finding the church, and then onto practicing my mediumship full time. The strange thing is, this never seemed odd. My involvement in mediumship felt like a natural process. And with synchronicity on my side, who was I to say no?

My first morning in the shop - now that felt a little different for me, as all the readings I had done before then were not for financial gain. I did them because I could and because the surroundings allowed for practice. At the shop, though, I was taking peoples' hard-earned money. I remember settling down into my little reading room and repeating over and over, "Spirit please be there, please be there." I almost went into a kind of repeated, exaggerated ritual of pleading and worthiness. By this time my nerves had complete hold of me and I was finding it hard to control my bladder. After my third trip to the bathroom the bell rang in my room to tell me my client was waiting down on the first floor where the shop was located.

Rounding up all my confidence I introduced myself to my first client. The appointment lasted 45 minutes. The time went so quick, and there it was, my first paid reading under my belt. I felt great. I loved my new job.

The speed at which my career came together and the lack of traditional training generally insisted upon in this movement was, and still is, one of my greatest assets. My relative lack of experience proved to me over and over that our ability to use our mediumship is a natural, instant process - if we chose to believe.

Not wanting to adopt the usual "It will take you one hundred years" development programmes offered in spiritualist churches, and being unwilling to accept that 33 years of life experience accounted for nothing, were choices I will never regret. I refused to believe that doing something so loving could be harmful to me if not practiced in the absolute same way as the last two hundred years' worth of ritual and chanting. My intent is good, which I believe can only bring good. That's a universal law, is it not?

As it turned out, the rebellious Reesy (that's me) started to grow a reputation because of his unorthodox approach to mediumship. Or perhaps I should say, the no hassle approach.

The way I saw it, if someone booked an appointment then that appointment was meant to be, end of discussion!

After some months in the shop, I found myself bouncing from one piece of advice to another (believe me, there are always eager volunteers who cannot wait to offer you their mediumistic experiences, advising the best way to link, open, close, protect and all the other make believe needs that they feel is necessary to emotionally and spiritually survive as a medium). I can't count the number of times I've been told that spirit will work you dead if you allow it, implying spirit doesn't care about rest for their workers. Believe me after my last job in the factory where the salary incentive schemes were enough to see off the strongest willed men, working with my mediumship was a breeze. And besides, this was the first time in my life I was working for myself. It's just great - I am my own boss, and if I decide to do overtime then that's my choice not spirits'. If anything, they have to reel me in and force me to rest.

So there I was, a complete novice about four months in and still confused due to all the free advice I was enduring from some of the most persistent people I had ever met. Before the shop, it was the church's loyal leaders, then came the keen armchair mediums that did very little but claimed to have travelled the world. I found myself wondering who to trust, who was correct, why should I have to follow all those rules and rituals... When I realized that constantly switching back and forth between advisors was much more exhausting than mediumship itself, I said, "Enough. It's time to let experience guide the way. Unless God appears in front of me and tells me otherwise, I'm going to trust myself and my simplistic way of working." Overnight my career in mediumship became less stressful. There was more flow and clarity in my readings. I took the same approach to my demonstrations and wow, even today I cannot thank myself enough.

Nonetheless, I knew there was still so much more I needed to understand about my mediumship. I was still very green as they say. I had heard of a college in Stansted, England, called the Arthur Findley College, which was named after the famous author Arthur Findley. The college, located in Findley's former home, is dedicated to teaching spirituality and psychic sciences. I decided to take the plunge and book myself a weeklong course. On arriving at the huge, historic mansion I was in awe at the size and energy of the building. Opening the large doors leading to the reception area was like an opening of energy - it was amazingly exciting. I was in a building full of potential mediums and the place was buzzing. It was very emotional as well because in some way it was as if I had come home. Why? What was I feeling? I was so relieved to be somewhere that I could gain a greater understanding of how mediumship would work for me. The thought kept repeating in my head, "At last it will all make sense for me."

At the welcome meeting, each teacher introduced his/herself and up stood Paul Jacobs - the man who would change my mediumship for the rest of my life. Paul's introduction to the group was, "If you come in my class you will work hard with no excuses." That was all I needed to hear! I was sold. The following morning, he began by demanding, "Okay, who's first to demonstrate in front of the class?" Well, I thought, what do I have to loose. I stood up on the stage and there she was, the first person I gave a message to that week was my future wife! I never expected to meet my wife, yet there she was, just stunning and what a fantastic medium. We spent the rest of the week flirting with each other at every given opportunity, and that was that, husband and wife.

Paul Jacobs is a no frills teacher medium who's style of instruction complemented my way of practicing my mediumship. He has no interest in the exaggerated traditions of mediumship and, being one of the most respected teacher mediums in Europe, meeting him was a life blessing in disguise. During that one week he gave me all the tools I had been seeking in order to continue building the foundation of my mediumship: realism, the belief in my simplistic approach, maturity and, above all else, the knowledge that I had made the correct choice in my new career. Thank you Paul Jacobs.

Back at home, I felt a new lease of confidence. After time I parted ways with the shop, always holding gratitude to Tracey and Rob for helping with the birth of my new career. Over the years to follow, I've tried to stay true to what I learned, working with dedication, a level head and, most of all, trust in the flow of my life.

Chapter 4

The Beginner: Keeping It Easy

This is my simple religion...
There is no need for temples.
There is no need for complicated philosophy.
Our own brain, our own heart is the temple.
The philosophy is loving, kindness and compassion.
                                        Dalai Lama b.1935

BEGINNER - wow! Never has a title been so overrated or overused with so little regard to the person it is being applied to. What is a beginner? The answer to this is, unfort-unately, not always positive, and may depend upon the organization to which you belong.

Is a beginner someone who has a few years of life under their belt, but needs a subtle reminder, or reawakening, of a sixth sense that has been suppressed by such hurdles as manipulation (of thoughts), beliefs instilled in childhood, and/or negative emotional or physical experiences? Or is a beginner someone who has many years ahead of them in which to prove his or herself? Both can apply, of course, and neither is bad, unless the individual starts out in an organization that insists one cannot fully develop his/her natural intuition until they're old enough to claim their personal retirement. You might feel the following paragraphs are harsh, but I am only speaking from personal experience. I have encountered many senior teachers in this business who insist that students move at a pace that is ridiculously slow, and therefore less threatening to their own ego. I have also met many students who express a total lack of confidence in the people they are meant to look up to and shear frustration at the lack of support within their organization. Debs and I have both seen people reduced to tears by bad advice, emotional bullying, and even blackmail. Yes, you read that correct: blackmail. Is that not illegal? Yet, believe me, it does occur.

The good news, of course, is that there are also some fantastic organizations out there that genuinely help students and newcomers. What is important is that you take your time deciding who is the best teacher for you and what is the best organization for you, as not all will fit your style or development or needs.

I have always believed that using intuition to link to loved ones passed over to spirit is something every person can do on a basic level. As I have said many times, this ability is not a gift; it is something we are each born with. It cannot be purchased, nor do we have to go to a school or university to learn its inner workings. The whole process of using your intuition, mediumship or psychic ability is as easy and natural as taking a breath in and exhaling out. | If this seems unlikely, ask yourself one question: Why would your loved ones in spirit wish it to be in any way difficult for you to make a loving link with them? The same goes for any link being made from any individual here on the living earth.

Unfortunately, this is not an opinion shared by everyone. I've gotten myself in deep water with many religious and spiritual teaching establishments due to my feelings on this subject. For too many people the idea that linking to spirit is something that we can all do with ease is unacceptable. The very thought of the everyday person becoming intuitive and able to make an evidential link to spirit overnight diminishes a lifetime of repetitive conviction that theirs is a gift. In order to justify all of their years of offering guidance (for some I would go as far as to say "manipulation"), such people must be correct. After all, they may say, they preach love and light and their intentions are always pure. Mmm... I'm not so convinced. Sorry, not from my experience.

The root of this problem is that any given person can set up business teaching and guiding others. Hey, I did the same myself: after several years of work, Debs and I decided to teach and so established Accolade Academy.

So, where am I going with this? Firstly, your intuition or mediumship is yours alone, it does not belong to anyone else. As such, it can never be at risk of fading or being taken away from you, even if you don't practice or develop your intuition or mediumship in a religious manner or under the guidance of a recognized teaching facility. It is yours. Remember that always. Secondly, everyone's mediumship is individual; no one can tell you exactly how it will, or should work. A teacher can only offer methods for ease of use or a point in the right direction, and only that when their morals are in the right place.

Let's keep this as simple as we possibly can. The foundations of your mediumship are no more than a feeling and a thought. We will look at the both individually in some detail, but first you have to promise that you will not allow your imagination to run wild. It can be so tempting to fall into the realm of dramatizing your mediumship beyond what it really is. So, let's hear it: "I promise to keep my mediumship real at all times." Okay, remember you promised and that promise is now a universal contract, no cheating. GOD IS WATCHING, as they say.

For ease of description I will use the word mediumship to cover all aspects of your intuition, sixth sense, psychic ability and spiritual evidential links throughout this book.

Feelings

There are many aspects of an individual's personality that can have a major influence on how his/her mediumship will function. These aspects of mediumship can vary enormously from person to person depending on his/her parental upbringing, religious background, and life experiences. Let's say as a child you were not allowed to express emotions, you were always told to stop crying or not show joy. You will have to work a little harder than someone who was allowed to express all emotions, as you would have learnt that allowing your feelings to extend themselves and become live was the wrong thing to do. After all, during our childhood, our mothers and fathers are always correct - children are taught to never question. All this means is that when you start to work with your feelings you will have to first accept that its okay to have emotions; get in touch with them, embrace them for what they need to express. The need to overcome instilled parental conditioning is not easy, but it is something you will be exposed to many times during your early days of development. Our emotions, happiness, sadness, excitement, regret, are a primary tool used by spirit to connect with us. They are the purest and most reliable form we have of communicating.

All aspects of your life have to be taken into consideration when developing for the first time. It is important that you trust your feelings and remain true to them, as they are your most loyal friends. They love you and always want what is best for you. They know you better than you know yourself, faults and all. The problem is that humans have, over the years, manipulated the whole process of relaying their true feelings to the point that we rarely voice what our true feelings mean for us to express thruthfully. For instance, how many times in life have you said the absolute opposite of what you were really feeling? This can be about anything in life no matter how small. Sometimes not saying exactly what we feel can seem like the best action to take in the moment, but if you do this too often you unknowingly start a new feeling language. This sounds strange, I know. What I am trying to say is that over time you develop new feelings to define your true or original feelings. Though these new, synthetic feelings are inauthentic, if you repeat the lie often enough, you create a believed reality that supersedes your true feelings. In a sense, you are being disloyal to yourself, and this disloyalty attracts negative karma. Yes, welcome to the world of truth.

What has this to do with your mediumship? Well, how many times have you observed a stranger while out and about, and found yourself developing a sense of that individual's personality (whether good or bad), but at the same time felt as if you were making that persona up? Truthfully, when making a link to a loved one in spirit, the situation is no different. When working, I get feelings that I recognize as a part of my life experiences; they are clearly my own, as I can recognize and express them in words. The only difference is that I have completely removed the synthetic, second feeling language when relaying my mediumship. Basically all I have done is discipline myself to recognize my true feeling language to the point that I am able to stay with it when working with my mediumship. This did not happen overnight. Rather it took time to remove 43 years of insecurities, because that is all synthetic feelings are: a form of insecurity or self-protection.

Once you adopt the mind-set of wanting to reopen your mediumship (remember, it's always been there), you then have to learn to trust the simplicity of the process. As you advertise your readiness to develop and experience your feelings to the universe and spirit, your emotions will open like a floodgate. Suddenly, you become a satellite dish. For as much as your emotions belong to you, you will have

volunteered them as one of your tools of communication. Please don't make this any more than what it is; I am talking about evidential mediumship here, not a huge mystic transition. All you will be doing is recognizing a feeling and then putting words to that feeling.
So, how will you know if you are making the feeling up or placing it there yourself by allowing your thoughts to run crazy? This knowledge will come with time and practice. In the meantime, remember that such things usually happen when you put too much pressure on yourself.

Do not be afraid of your emotions. Sometimes, when working, I become so overrun with an emotion I can't get my words out due to the intensity. I often feel like I am about to start crying. What I have learned is that this is not my doing, as these times of intensity do not relate to anything happening at that moment, and in real terms I would have no reason to feel such emotion other than for the benefit of the message and my mediumship.

I cannot explain your feeling language, as everyone's emotions and their meanings are different. It is necessary that you work this one out for yourself. I've found the following method helpful. Sit with a friend and relay what you are truly feeling about that person. I don't mean your personal opinions about his/her personality or habits, but more so your compassionate feelings. What do you feel your friend has had to overcome in life? Do they feel happy or sad because of those events? Has your friend experienced a loss of a loved one? Trust your own feelings, and relay them to your friend in words. Always remember you are relaying a message using your most compassionate feelings for that person. The word FOR is very important here, because the moment you allow your personal feelings to become biased in any way, or the moment you make a personal judgment, the experience will fail. What do I mean by this? Say it becomes clear that your friend may like to spend her downtime with a hobby that you would never entertain. Although you don't tell your friend that would be a hobby you would never participate in yourself, you may very subtly manipulate your feelings, in this case by advising your friend not to continue with that hobby just because personally it would not be your choice. At that moment you have allowed your feelings to become biased within the reading when delivering the message in its truest sense.

In mediumship, it is important to remember that although you are using your feelings to relay a message or evidential mediumship, it has nothing to do with you - you are a messenger and nothing more. You see, too many mediums become too opinionated when delivering messages, allowing their personal views on the client's life or where the client is/should be in life to supersede the true message they are receiving from spirit - similar to what I've stated above. As a medium you have a responsibility to keep your personal opinions to yourself. You are delivering a message for a loved one in spirit, not from your personal bank of biased experiences. Remember, what you say can have a life-changing effect on your client. It is equally important to remember that linking to spirit should always be a positive action, never negative. In all my years of reading I have never felt the need to give anything that is so negative as to cause distress for a client. I'm sorry, that's not my role. I'm just Paul Rees, not God.

Mediumship is the most obvious language you will encounter. For instance, how do I know, during a session, that I have someone's father with me from spirit? Because spirit will give me a sense that feels like a Dad to me. Not my Dad, but much the same. You see, in order to know the relationship of your spirit contact, you will be given the feeling of someone you have experienced in your life. A grandmother will feel like your grandmother feels, or felt, to you. The intensity of this feeling will vary, depending upon the similarities. For instance, if the spirit contact's personality was similar to your grandmother's, certain trademarks of your grandmother's personality will be heightened so that you can recognize and relay such traits to the client (as part of the spirit's personality description). Otherwise, the intensity will be fairly light.

These are the basics of how your feelings might allow you to recognize spirit relationships. Now, let's go a few steps further. What if you have someone's brother in spirit, but you have never had a brother in real life. In this situation, you may wonder how is it you can feel something you have never experienced in your lifetime. This is when you must rely on your imagination. We all have the ability to call upon imaginary, or remembered, feelings. Unlike the synthetic feelings discussed above, which are disloyal and therefore misleading, your imaginary feelings are harmless, much the same as those experienced when playing make believe as a child. I remember staging war games with my friends. Whenever my team won, I got flutters in my tummy as we celebrated, thinking we were like true soldiers on the battlefield. When called upon to relay that type of evidence to my client, I use those remembered feelings to describe good times in school or with friends.

We can go even further with this.

I have, in past readings, given evidence to clients of spirit contacts who were stabbed or died in shootings or from suicide by hanging, to name just a few. Because I have never in real life experienced the feelings of any of these events, all I can do is image what such things would feel like. I have, like everyone, accumulated a bank of feelings through the visual teachings of my life - from reading, watching television, and going to the cinema. Feelings are very powerful; allow yourself to flow with them when working. You should never have to give them too much thought, as relaying such feelings for the message should be instantaneous. If you find yourself stalling - wondering what a certain feeling means to you - then this is generally because you have allowed yourself to get in the way of the process. In other words, you have, in some way, brought in your own judgment, or tried to make sense of the evidence you are giving. Do not allow yourself to become in any way critical; this is not your role, and we are not here to judge.

Thoughts

This process is a little easier to describe, and therefore trust, as the average person has not spent a lifetime manipulating their thoughts in the same way as we do feelings. A thought is a thought; some we hear louder than others, some we recognize quicker than others, and some appear very visual.

We will start with the basics. How do thoughts work in your mediumship? How do you know the thoughts you convey are not your thoughts? Recognizing the difference generally comes with your intent at that given moment, just like any other basic action we carry out in life. What you have to do is make a conscious shift in your mind to have thoughts from spirit for your client. This becomes the reality and your thoughts are now part of your evidential mediumship. Let's say you have something cooking in the oven and it's ready to be removed. On approaching the oven, you shift your intent from whatever it was you were just doing to the task before you. This brings awareness to the danger of hot surfaces and the fact that you need oven gloves. The oven has now become your primary thought and nothing will supersede that.

The thoughts that come to you while working will most definitely feel like your own. The process will feel very natural and easy, like the unfolding of a story. Some thoughts are very obvious and some very subtle. What you will recognize over time is the value of each thought. For instance, the varying intensity of some thoughts can ensure that you recognize, collect, and deliver all the evidence and messages that your spirit contact intended you to receive and pass on to your client or audience. And remember what I said about loud and subtle thoughts? As a rule of thumb, a loud thought is what I like to call a highlighter. Just like the brightly coloured pens we use to visibly emphasize text on paper or screen, they are there to highlight a subject your spirit link wishes you to concentrate upon.

Putting it All Together

Now, let's discuss how this will work in your mediumship. Say the first thought that comes to mind is a loud thought that says, "train driver." At the same time, you may have a feeling of a grandfather. There's your start - you know you have a grandfather who was possibly a train driver or worked on the railway while here on Earth. As time goes on and with practice, you will learn what thoughts are yours and what thoughts are spirit's. In turn, this knowledge will enable you to recognize when you are subtly sabotaging your link with erroneous or judgmental thoughts.

Taking the time to recognize and acknowledge each one is important. As I've stated above, a loud thought is a highlighter. Highlighters are very obvious thoughts, in that you almost want to shout them out, as they feel so prominent in your mind. Don't be tempted to move on to your next loud thought until you completely finish with this one. Remember, a highlighter is a major player, the one that gets your attention and allows you access to a certain place in the spirit contact's life. Returning to the grandfather and train driver: the train driver thought is the highlighter. Its appearance is your prompt to work with the subtler thoughts and feelings that come with this highlighter. For instance, perhaps a subtler thought will suggest the spirit contact once worked on the railway. Basically the subtle thoughts provide your quality evidence.

With both loud and subtle thoughts, visuals will appear in your mind's eye. For me, these are just like pictures, visuals of places, actual words and so on, and are intended to complement your feelings and subsequent thoughts. Names also come as visuals in my mind's eye, and this can be the same for other types of evidence. Over time what happens is that all three - feelings, thoughts, and visuals - come to work in sync with one another, constantly feeding your evidence and creating a harmonious balance for easy connections and quality of evidence and service. In the beginning, you may stop and start, have pauses of panic, or get yourself all in a mess due to a lack of experience. Know that only you can stop a communication; spirit will never leave you adrift, and your loyalty will never be disrespected in any way.

Just take your time; you don't have to be fluent to be understood and a message containing forty words can be just as powerful and meaningful as a message of four thousand words. Remember this: mediums are not great, just experienced.

Chapter 5
My Self-Analysis

As important as it is to have confidence, it's also important to recognize why you must work on that confidence, for it is made up of the life-instilled rules and regulations that play a role in your approach to, and belief system around, your mediumship. This exercise asks that you acknowledge the negative thoughts, those we keep hidden away, in order to make room for the positive.

Think about your childhood roles and experiences and the negative beliefs that you developed about yourself. These can seriously affect the way you work! What personality traits do you feel may have held you back when working? Which do you feel hinder the start to your new development? For example, do you suffer a lack of self-esteem or a sense of not being good enough for mediumship? The responsibility for what you say - Why would anyone listen to me? What if I get it wrong? Will I appear over-confident, or a show off? - lies within.

These are only a few of the traits that can stop a good medium in his or her tracks. Take a look inside and see what might be stopping you from shining. Complete this exercise periodically, copying these pages as needed.

For Your Notes

Date:

My Notes of Truth:

My Negative Beliefs:

My Personal Challenges:

Positive Outcomes

Chapter 6

Your Mediumship: The Starting Block, Responsibility, and Your Product

Turn your vision inward and the whole world will be full of supreme spirit.
                    Ramana Maharshi 1879 - 1950

In this section we will look at getting started, working responsibly, and effective ways to brand yourself as the product.

The Starting Block

There are so many questions as you begin working with your mediumship. Can I do this? Do I have the ability to link to spirit? Will it be easy? To these questions, we answer: yes, yes, and yes (sort of)!

As stated at the onset, Debs and I believe that we all have the ability to link to spirit or give an evidential link to a client/recipient that validates a loved one from spirit by communicating a memory to that client/recipient. This process is not rocket science in any way. As you open senses that have lain dormant, waiting to be used in their truest sense, you will be surprised at the truth of this statement. Are mediums closer to God or Spirit? No. Are they more sensitive than the average person? Yes, but only because they have worked and practised to become so - just as you can, just as anybody can. As you read through this book you will see the word "Trust" many times, as this is a key ingredient in your mediumship toolbox. If you are totally new and want to start developing your intuition, the key will be to never over-inflate your expectations. Relaying evidence of a loved one who has passed over to spirit to a client is an enfoldment of a memory (or memories) that will be accompanied by feelings similar to nostalgia or déjà vu; a feeling you will recognize almost as your own.

In beginning your mediumship career, your first mindful choice comes in the form of an answer to an important question: What kind of psychic/medium do you want to be? Do you want to be the same as the millions already available, large portions of which give the same brand of generic evidence? Choosing this path may be quicker, but in doing so, you will step into an already saturated market that has a deservedly poor reputation. After all, any fool can deliver a message, as is proven hourly in many of the psychic "call centres" around the world. Let's assume, however, that is not the path you want to take. You can have a prosperous career as a dedicated, skilled and knowledgeable medium if you stay focused and aim always to deliver honest evidence that's unquestionable to the recipient. All of Accolade's students are taught from the offset of their development that getting and giving finely detailed evidence of a contact from spirit is an absolute priority. I'm talking about details that deliver the WOW factor and leave critics slack-jawed. How great will it be to not just say you have someone's Mom, Dad, Son, Daughter, Aunty, Uncle, etc. in spirit, but to name that individual and give birth dates, life details and so on. Now that's what we call a message! Decide now to be the medium who delivers and I promise the psychic-message portion of your links will always be both credible and detailed.

Your Responsibility in Mediumship

In reaching for little more than success and fame, many psychics/mediums forget their responsibilities to their profession. The following are a few tips to keep you on the right track in terms of a healthy mediumship. Your first responsibility is to promise yourself from the start that you will always put the client first and use every opportunity available to look deeper and search for greater evidence and validation of loved ones passed. Keep in mind always - it's great to be busy but not at the cost of the quality of your service. Study your conscience, and make sure you know where your morals lie. I have seen a trend emerge in many established spiritual camps all over the world in the last few years where resident mediums claim clients are only searching for spiritual counselling and no longer wish validation of loved ones in spirit. Such workers often change their advertised title from "psychic medium" to "psychic councellors." I have no idea who decided this was the path forward, because it is not what Debs and I are hearing from the clients we've encountered in our own work. The trend is, I fear, little more than a method meant to fit the needs of lazy workers and fill greedy pockets.

At some point in our lives we all need some guidance, and yes that part of the medium message is very important, but I would be dammed if I, as a client, would ever be happy accepting such guidance without sound evidence as to who it is that the worker is communicating with. Globally, human expectations are geared towards getting value for our money, and I don't believe clients can, or should, be bullied into accepting less. Keep you morality healthy and the universe will always reward you. Remember owning a good intent is a true motivator in life.

Your second responsibility comes in the form of a piece of advice: the less you know, the easier working within your mediumship will be. There are many stories about psychics and mediums who research evidence prior to readings in order to have advanced knowledge about their client(s). This is the same as a death wish as far as your career is concerned, and not only because such practices are cheating. The truth is, the less you know the easier it is to prevent your own thoughts from manipulating the evidence. We will touch on this later in the book. I always tell clients before I start any appointment - the only answers I require while offering evidence is "yes" or "no," unless I ask otherwise.

Finally, it is important to note, your mediumship will not be enough to sustain your career, as crazy as that sounds. You are selling an emotion and, in many cases, a memory. As such, you always have to carry the desire to do your best, have pride in your work, sympathy, empathy, respect and, most of all, patience. Always remember who pays you and why; your services are truly deserving of payment and being paid well for your dedication is no crime to God or spirit, but never take it for granted!

Your Product and Your Profile

You are the medium, the product, and the profile all in one. Your job is to sell yourself as well as your mediumship. Your image, your approach to your clients (regardless of how difficult - remember the customer is king), and your personality will all play a huge role in the making of your career. You have to be warm and empathetic, as you are sharing and divulging some of you clients' most personal memories.

How exciting is your work to watch? What makes you stand out from the millions of other mediums working? What makes your services exceptional? These are just a few essential questions you need to ask yourself before starting your career.

All products have a shelf life, and all working mediums are products. No matter how good a medium you are, in order to maintain customer confidence, you must also be generous and true to those seeking your services.

Staying current and relevant is another must. Many mediums allow themselves to get caught in an invisible time warp, insisting that older (out dated) methods are best. Still others use an antiquated vocabulary that fell from usage many moons ago. Work hard to keep all aspects of your mediumship fresh and up to date, including your business presentation. How fresh is the artwork in your ads, business cards, etc.? How pleasing to the eye is your logo? Does it scream "old news" to potential customers? I have seen hundreds of cards and advertisements that feature the perfect blue sky or lake, mountains, butterflies, rainbows, and/or the exhausted colour purple! DON'T GO THERE! Give your artwork some thought, remembering that sometimes less is better. Your business cards and artwork should complement forward-thinking attitudes and practices, not those of the past.

Your profile can also be an invisible gift from the client to you in that a good profile will result in a rise in public status that transfers the energy of appreciation, respect, and gratitude like an uplift of your stardom being passed from one client to the next. This creates what the media call a "buzz" - which wonderful sense of urgency new clients will have to come and see you work. This buzz is akin to silent applause or a hidden thank you, and often gets taken for granted by many high profile mediums. Always remember this silent uplift is as fragile as it is strong and it depends upon remembering who it was that got you and your career to that level: your profile and your clients.

When the medium fails to respect the profile freely given by his/her loyal customers, it will diminish at a pace unnoticeable until it's too late. Remember prevention is better than cure as they say.

So there you have it a few easy thoughts that are worth their weight in gold if respected by the worker and used with good intention. Go for it!

Chapter 7
My Quarterly Self-Assessment

It is important to periodically acknowledge and record any new sensitivity, feelings and thoughts you notice. For instance, are you giving new evidence in your readings and demonstrations? Why or why not? Do you recognise any new repetitive working habits? If so, make notes focused on removing them. Also make notes of the highlights from your last quarter. Enjoy the act of writing them, and praise yourself. It's good to have a healthy ego. Make your assessments as detailed as you can. As noted, in order to be effective this exercise should be completed on a quarterly basis. Copy these pages as necessary.

1st Quarter Self-Assessment
Date:

Notes:

1st Quarter Self-Assessment
Date:

Notes:

2nd Quarter Self-Assessment
Date:

Notes:

3rd Quarter Self-Assessment
Date:

Notes:

4th Quarter Self-Assessment
Date:

Notes:

Chapter 8

My Analogy; Your Understanding!

I started my life with a single absolute: that the world was mine to shape in the image of my highest values and never to be given up to a lesser standard, no matter how long or hard the struggle.

Ayn Rand

I often use analogies to describe the most efficient ways to make the most of our mediumship. The car analogy is one of my favourites because an automobile is built to do whatever you tell it to do, responding the very second you ask it to - whether you ask it to speed up, slow down, turn or keep you entertained. As crazy as it sounds, if what you want is to crash the car, then you can. It is the same for your mediumship.

Let's say your mediumship is a car, one of the finest available on the market today with the added bonus that it will never become dated or old. I mean oh, what a car, self-servicing and everlasting.

The moment you decide to direct energy or thought to your mediumship, it is ready to go - just like putting your foot on the accelerator. You are in control of how fast or slow you wish your mediumship to cruise. As with the car, the heavier the foot on the accelerator the faster it goes. You are responsible for the control of the car. Again, the same is true for your mediumship, only instead of using your foot to accelerate you use confidence, belief and self-love. You see, your mediumship is the perfect means of transportation, never concerned with its surroundings, at ease in any condition, and ready to obey your commands. But remember, this is only true if you believe it to be.

Each time you put your medium brakes on due to a decline in self-confidence, then so shall your mediumship slow or be weakened. This is not the decision of your mediumship; it is yours alone. You see, going back to the car analogy - a car will not stop or slow unless you create a corresponding action. Just easing your foot off the accelerator slows the car; for many, this is such a reflexive manoeuvre it goes almost unnoticed. Again the same is true for your mediumship. You may well be sabotaging your ability on a level that you fail to notice, for we are a proud species. Hiding behind a shield of stubbornness, many of us are reluctant to say when our pride has been hurt or our self-confidence knocked.

It is important that you learn to recognize the personal weaknesses that set you back within your mediumship. Often, it's too easy to blame others. That's not to say there are not difficult clients out there, as there are many, but hey, that's life. You don't hear the car moaning each time you take it out in the rain.

Which brings us to medium/psychic working conditions. Over the years I have seen many a great medium fail due to uneasiness and nerves over how he/she felt about a given working venue. Perhaps it was not the near-perfect environment needed for the medium to be able to carry out his/her demonstrations or to do individual one to one readings. I can sympathize with this, as it's commonplace to work in clubs or pubs and bars in the UK and we all know -

the more alcohol consumed the louder the audience becomes. Debs and I have had to work in venues where fights have broken out on the very same table the client to whom we were linking with sat, or in venues where the music was so loud that we could hardly hear ourselves think yet alone work. Why do we do it? And why should you? There are many reasons. For one, our aim is to reach people who generally would not attend a church or spiritual centre. This is important because if we only preach to the converted, then Accolade, mediumship and spiritualism will remain stuck within the confines of one belief system, never growing in any way.

Secondly, as teacher mediums, it's our job to put ourselves in working environments that are more challenging than the usual. That way we can then take our experiences into the classroom to help our students. It is important not to kid yourselves and think you will always have the serenity of a near perfect working environment, as today's society does not carry the respect of fifty years ago. As I have said to all of our students over the years: it does not matter where the venue, what the noise level, how tough the surroundings, or any other issue that might disturb your work - such complaints do not justify the excuses happily used to explain poor mediumship. A lack of understanding for your need to create the perfect environment for an audience or client is irrelevant. "YOU CAN DO IT," I tell them. You can work no matter the situation. GO FOR IT. These are times of inner strength, with opportunities to build your self-confidence. This newly gained confidence will then naturally compliment your mediumship.

Like you, it took me some time to understand why I had to accommodate difficult clients and venues, but without such experiences, I would not be the medium I am today. As in any other job, repetitive work means repetitive mediumship. So ask yourself - what kind of medium do I wish to be? The everyday same-same, or something special? To be different you have to push yourself beyond your comfort areas. If you are going to grow your clientele, you will have to reach people that generally don't get reached. (That is of course if that's your aim within your mediumship. If not, no worries sit back and enjoy.)

Always remember, as a working medium you are open to criticism. Repeated statements or evidence from yourself will gain the attention of your clients, eroding their faith in your ability to get fresh evidence. Growth is an expectation from a client's first visit to his or her subsequent visits. Maintaining good momentum is the secret, so keep your foot hard on the gas and remember, your car is perfect and you are the perfect driver.

Chapter 9
You Are the Technician

Nothing is lost that we do not first see as lost. Visions born of fear give birth to our failing. Visions born of hope give birth to our success. What is possible lives within us, and it only remains for us to discover it.

Terry Brooks

In mediumship, as in all areas of life, intent can be our strength and our weakness. What we often forget is that our intentions create much of our in-the-moment reality. In that way, it is much like a cat: it thinks in the now and can be loyal in both a positive and a negative sense. Which it will be, positive or negative, depends on you, the technician.

Your intent is there for you to use as you wish; it has no preferences, but it does have lightning fast reactions that go unseen to the human eye. Now, that's what I call a James Bond 007-style weapon! The only difference being that intent is personal; it can only work on you because it is your intention that creates the action that corresponds to your desire or reluctance to follow through with a personal experience of any kind. As with all weapons, your intent deserves all the respect and recognition you can gather, as it is the most potentially damaging and rewarding tool in your mediumship box.

This is the device you will use over your lifetime to convince yourself of both your weaknesses and your strengths. That's why I call it the "can I" or "can't I" do it tool. As the technician, it is important to remember your intent is your responsibility; its use has nothing to do with spirit. Because your reality affects your clients, you must pay attention to how you care for your intent: feed it negative thoughts and it will grow negatively, feed it positive thoughts and it will grow positively.

Intent is subtle, and yet it is in charge of creating or destroying self-confidence - which we have already established as being vital to your mediumship. Let's look at an example. Perhaps a great one to use would be the intent to take better care of ourselves, as we have all made this resolution at some point in our lives. We decide in December to wait for January to start an exercise program as part of a new year/new start project. The New Year's deadline comes and goes without exercise. January comes and goes without exercise. What happened? When making this promise to ourselves, we were full of energy and enthusiasm, with confidence to match. What changed between the day we made the promise to ourselves and January was our intent. YES the subtle effect of intent changed your planned new project from a positive experience to a negative one, allowing you to grow the conviction that it's okay to not follow through with an intended action. In this way, forward motion is blocked, replaced by a self-granted permission to lose to oneself yet again.

So let's apply this scenario to the everyday development of the working medium. Say you book a seat in a workshop four months in advance. You feel good, confident. A few months pass and it gets a little closer to the workshop start date. You begin to get a little twitchy in your tummy. It's still okay though, you have a few weeks to prepare. Suddenly it's the night before the workshop and the nerves are running high.

You ask yourself, why did I book this workshop. Can I get out of it? Then you start looking for excuses: do I have time to give up the whole weekend for this? Can I afford to lose the money I've paid out? This is where you need to stop and think about what you are telling yourself and the universe: "When I booked the workshop, I felt I was good enough to attend. Now I don't."

But WHY? What's changed for you? I have had students pull out on the morning of a workshop due to nerves, and believe me I've heard every excuse possible.

You are your mediumship. You are your intent, you are your actions, and you are your thoughts. This is common knowledge for most and something we teachers are all very quick to preach. Your mediumship totally relies on you and your belief that you can make it happen; the belief that the contact from spirit to you has always and will always be there for you in its full potential. Feeding your intent on negativity is all it takes to stop this belief and your mediumship in their tracks.

For ease of understanding, let's break down both positive and negative intent a bit further.

Negative Intent

Negative intent is caused by the self-doubt that appears, often from fright and nerves, before participating in any activity that you know you can do or which you have done in the past. These doubts come when you're asked to perform under pressure, and can, if you allow them to, result in your completely backing out or allowing others to go before you so you can judge by comparison and play it safe. This, by the way, will bring you karma, as it also creates negativity towards others.

When we are teaching in workshops, I ask students to volunteer for exercises. Too often, I can almost guarantee that most will give off energy that says, "OH MY GOD, we have to work!" They came to the class to learn, but suddenly they blame that very thing for their lack of confidence! Why? I've come to recognize this as a move students use to mask their change of intent from positive to negative. At the same time, they feel a need to cover up their lack of confidence from the other students - so, out come the excuses. If it's a morning workshop, the favourite is, "It's too early for me to work." Placement of negative intent doesn't have to be an outright statement, however. It can be something as subtle as a roll of the eyes, a sense of not wanting to be there, a silent judgment of your own ability. And it can take effect even before you make the journey to the workshop. That's when the overwhelming need you've put on yourself strikes, causing you to ask spirit to be there for you during the day ahead, repeating this plea over and over, and maintaining this thought throughout the day. This manifests as the fear that you will get no evidence from spirit when asked to work randomly in front of the class.

This list of excuses is endless and just what your negative intent loves, so let's look at ways to change negative intent to:

Positive Intent

After a little practice, you will be amazed how easy it is to maintain a positive intent. All it takes is a little self-confidence and you'll be up and running. Generally your intent is weakened by fear, usually to do with another person's skill or experience as compared to your own. If this is the case, remind yourself, it does not take an Einstein to be a medium. This is a career for anybody in any walk of life. I tell myself over and over during my work: if the next person can do this, then I can do it too. What makes any other professional medium any different to me? Nothing. The ability to be a good medium is free, with no special gifts needed other than the patience to gain experience and the willingness to work on self-development. (Both of which are true for most roles in life.) For example, we all have the same emotions, senses and other creative abilities needed to fit the bill of a medium. There is a common misperception that all mediums are born super-sensitives, angelic beings that differ from the everyday person. Well, this is not the case. You have a choice as to how sensitive you wish to become in your intuition, which improves through practice and self-belief. So there it is. You simply say, "I'm a medium." Why does it have to be any harder than that?

It doesn't, provided you maintain a positive intent. Positive intent has to come from the inside, however. It's a discipline that you will need as you practice your mediumship, and it comes from confidence that only you can provide. This is not part of a ten-year plan, either. Confidence can be an overnight change if that's what you want. Listen I did it: I gave myself the intent to develop and practice my mediumship in a positive way that insisted upon rapid self-growth. How can you do this? The answer is two-fold. First, tell yourself there will be no backing out. And second, always volunteer to go first. For me this wasn't from a desire to be the first. Rather, it was my way of keeping on top of my positive intent. This is still the main discipline I use today. Just go for it every time! Say to yourself: if I'm here, then this is meant to be.

Remember the very moment you give yourself chicken nerves and allow yourself to back out or allow others to take your place, you are telling the universe you are not good enough. Immediately, that element of positive intent will be exchanged for negative intent - all under your instruction. Then you will have to work that much harder to regain that positive intent.
My motto is, "Keep your positive intent close and strong." You've worked too damn hard to let it go. A positive intent

conforms to the shape of your soul, whilst a negative intent creates only sharp edges.

Chapter 10
My Awakening

Your vision will become clear only when you look into your heart. Who looks outside...dreams. Who looks inside... awakens.
                                    Carl Jung 1875 - 1961

Firstly I need to let the reader know that I am not, nor do I profess to be, an expert on scientific or spiritual matters. Some of the theories I put forth in this book are my own, and consist of what makes sense to my mind and spiritual senses. Others theories are based upon my life journey of the last ten years, which has included extensive study of the vast amounts of literature available regarding the spiritual, scientific, religious, and the newly adopted "channelled" explanations for our existence. Theories presented by others based on their personal and professional experiences of mediumship have also played a major part in my coming to the conclusions I put forth. I do not profess to have all of the answers on these subjects. Nor do I believe any living person possesses the one "truth," or all of the answers to all of the questions regarding our origins or of the processes of life and what we call the afterlife.

I cannot for sure say that I was even aware of spirit until I was 25 years old. Although magical, the encounter I had at that time was very brief. I believe not having any contact from spirit as a child was due in part to my upbringing, particularly in the first five years of my life. My Dad was a priest in 1950's Ireland. Due to personal abuse, he ran away from the priesthood at twenty years old, carrying with him huge amounts of guilt and shame. Having absconded from the priesthood, and therefore God, I believe he was frightened out of his mind of the consequences he thought he would face upon death. As a result, my knowledge of the afterlife and what it meant was very scary in my early years. When angry, Dad shouted at us, "You're going to hell," or "The devil is going to get you." One of his favourite sayings was, "I see the devil in your eye." His words were accompanied by much violence, which caused me to develop an all-consuming terror of the afterlife that I tried desperately to shut out. This was during my first few years of life and so made a huge impress-ion on my little mind.

I don't blame my father, for this was what he was taught, what he himself had gone through as a child. Though I must say that coming to this conclusion of forgiveness is the result of much healing on my part.

After many years of wandering through life, at 25 I went against my better judgment and went to a medium. Looking back now, I know exactly why I went. Yet at the time I had no idea, I just knew I needed to go.

I was not in a very good place, as it was emotionally one of the worst times of my life. As I entered the medium's house, I was again consumed by terror, just as I had been as a little girl. All my fears came back to haunt me at once. As it happens, I never did have a reading that day. The medium was a lovely lady and very understanding; she decided that because of my emotional state, I was too fragile for a reading and that I would benefit more from spiritual healing. Spiritual healing is when a living person asks for healing energy from spirit to come and surround them, allowing them to pass on energy through their hands to the person in need of healing.

So there I was, kneeling on the medium's living room floor, suffering a panic attack. She placed her hands on my forehead. Because I had never heard of spiritual healing, this didn't help my panic attack one little bit. What were her hands doing on my head? I was in the middle of one of the worst times in my life, terrified and feeling so alone in that terror. As I lifted my head to ask the medium to stop healing me, I looked up. There across the room, appearing as clear as the medium and myself, was an old lady in a long, floating lilac dress. She had a kind face that wore a soft smile. To this day I believe she was my father's mother, Mary McEnroe. She was my Irish Nana, and I had never met her. I saw just one photograph of her, and that was how she looked in the photograph, now more healthy and relaxed. I looked at her beautiful dress; lowering my gaze I could see that both she and her dress kind of disappeared three quarters of the way down, like she had no legs below the knee. It was as if the image had run out of energy and so she was hovering. You would have definitely thought that this experience would have made me worse, but the sight of her seemed to calm me down. She had a small bunch of flowers in her hand and I instinctively knew they were for me.

I acknowledged her and soaked up everything about her in my mind; only then did she disappear. All told I must have looked at her for only seconds, not long at all but long enough to know that the vision was real and long enough for her image to be imprinted on my mind. Even now, fifteen years later, I can still recall in detail all that she was as if I am seeing her before me. That I was able to see her then felt unusual, yet totally natural. Although I was looking at her standing across the room, I was also aware that the real image of her was in my mind. It was as if my mind was the projector where the image really lived, and it extended out into the room like a hologram. That is the best analogy I can give you to explain how it felt to see her.

That was my first real encounter with spirit. I came away from the medium's house more relaxed than I had felt in years. Yet it would not be for another five years that I would become interested in mediumship and the afterlife.

Some two years after my lovely spirit-lady appeared, I started seeing lights. I saw these objectively, meaning outside of myself. They were bright little lights, varying in size. Some were the size of a coaster that you rest your cup on. Others were the size of a fifty pence piece, with all the sizes in between. They lasted just a second and then they disappeared. They also came in all different colours, though mainly purple, blue, pink and white. Every light had just one colour.

This often happened while I was in a room by myself, while watching TV or reading. They appeared across the room from me, never close to me or around my person. Yet there were times when I caught them around other people when they were talking to me, always from the shoulders up, never below. Again they would last a second and be gone.

I am not suggesting that these lights are normal or abnormal phenomena that occur for others in the beginning of their development. What are they then? In truth I do not know for sure, but here are my theories:

I believe what I saw with my naked eye were orbs. Orbs are considered to be the energy of spirits. They are mainly captured on photographs; if you zoom in to the orb, you can sometimes see a human face within.

This did not happen all the time. Sometimes I wouldn't see one for a week, then I would see three in one day. I also believe that my guides used this as a way of getting my attention, awakening me to spirit, as they were unobtrusive, non-threatening, warming little lights of pretty colours, perfect for scared little Debs, yet eye catching and unusual enough to call notice.

This was a wonderful way to get me to notice them, and to awaken me to spirit without any risk of putting me off. At that time, even at the age of 27, I still found anything to do with spirit frightening. Childhood scars are not quick to heal, and even as an adult, I could be at a friend's house and have to leave with yet another panic attack caused by the emergence of Tarot cards. As you see, spirit really had to be careful with me, as I was very fragile in all areas of my life, let alone this area. Yet awakened I had to be.

Is it normal to see lights objectively when first starting out with your development? No not as a rule. Can it be expected within development? Again no, not expected but it is possible, of course, as it happened to me. I am not a special person. I have no more to me than does the person next to me. Were the lights necessary for me? Most definitely!

I have since discovered that when I am conducting private readings, I sometimes see these lights, and that they are my cue to ask the recipient if they see them. They always answer yes, that they see them as well. I am then able to tell the recipient that it is my belief that these lights are the spiritual energy of a loved one who has passed over.

I do not believe that there is one hard and fast rule to development or to an individual's awakening. Some people do not need to be awakened, as they have grown up accustomed to spirituality and mediumship through relatives who are workers or spiritual church attendees, etcetera. I needed the lights, many will not, and still others will have experiences that I did not.

Spirit to my mind, does not present itself as entertainment. If you are a level-headed, grounded person with a strong sense of who you are, then very little may be needed to encourage you to sign up as it were, and start your development. Some of us need to be handled with care, as if we have a fragile sign on our spiritual box so spirit will know to open the box carefully. It all depends on where we sit in our lives to start with. What I do know is that spirit will not appear for just any little reason, as that would eliminate the need for us to come to our own conclusions about life and the afterlife. This is, after all, a major reason why we incarnate in the first place. Enlightenment HAS to be an inner journey. If spirit showed up all over the place, we could hardly have this journey.

I should say that at first I didn't take any notice of the lights, which I now think is pretty weird. Why did I not think to go to the optician or the doctor? Then one day I saw one of the lights and, before I could even think about it, I said aloud to an empty room, "Please go away. I am not ready yet." Hmm, very weird again. Who was I asking to go away? What was I not ready for? Also, what did I mean by "yet"? Perhaps they listened: as it happened I didn't see any spiritual lights for another two years. They left me alone, as I had asked.

By the time I started seeing the lights again, I had returned to the medium I saw a few years before. By this time I'd been through much counselling, which I can only assume she was relieved to hear. I had also started to read books on self-help, great books that complemented my healing. As I unloaded much of the baggage I had carried around since childhood, I found myself opening to the spiritual side of life, as many of the books I had read made reference to spiritual practices. I believe the turning point came when I attended an eight-day residential retreat in Brighton, called The Hoffman Process. These are available all over the world and were started by a great man named Bob Hoffman, from California. This was the first time I had been involved in a practical way with anything spiritual. The experience was very loving, and for the first time in my life I felt safe within it. After that I did not look back.

One day, not long after my Hoffman experience, I found out about and ordered Psychic News, where I immediately saw an advertisement for The Arthur Findlay College of Psychic Science. I decided that I had to get there, no matter what.
I fell in love with the college, and spent one week a month there for the next eighteen months. In this time my mediumship grew enormously along with my confidence. And my confidence not only grew within my mediumship but also within my relationship with the spiritual side of life.

In one of my courses at Arthur Findlay, I saw a handsome little Welshman who not only caught my eye, but also my heart. His name was Paul Rees. Little did I know at the time he would be my future husband.

My first demonstration was part of a Wednesday evening service in the Sanctuary at the college. Not only do all of the students, but also teachers and members of the public attend. I remember sitting in the dining room at about 6:00pm. My teacher came up to me while I was having dinner and stated that I had been chosen to give a student demonstration that evening at the service. Well talk about start as you mean to go on! I pushed my dinner aside, feeling so stressed that I thought for sure I might return to spirit myself. My cheeks burnt bright red, and all I wanted to do was leave. Everything in me, every fiber of my being, was heightened, as if I had been switched to hyperactive duty. I could not get a sensible thought together in my head.

I spent the remainder of the time before the service began, at 7:30pm, in the toilet unable to calm my nerves.

At 7:30, I sat on the platform of the Sanctuary, asking God to please take me home, anything so I didn't have to do the demonstration. I wondered why in God's name anyone ever put him or herself through such stress.

When my name was called, I stood up with not a thought in my head. All was blank. As I walked to the front of the platform and looked out at the sea of faces staring back at me, my entire being had a sense of, "How on Earth will I do this."
I needn't have worried. I had been instructed I was to give only two communications. The two loved ones from spirit who came through to me to be recognized were easy to work with; there weren't too many 'no's from recipients and not a single long pause. I felt that the links were quite good, and I was proud of myself not only for the work I'd done, but also for the courage I had shown.

In the first year following this experience, I did many demonstrations in Spiritualist churches, though I only conducted the odd one to one reading. I found there to be seven churches in my hometown alone, my first demonstration being in a church called Totton in Southampton. During this demonstration, I felt no different to the way I had at the Arthur Findlay College. I had exactly the same anxieties, the same stresses. This anxiety lasted about two years as I developed. I could not eat two days before a demonstration and found it hard to concentrate on anything else. No one could make me feel better, no matter what they said. I would suffer so much. I constantly threw up. Most people probably would have given up. Why put yourself though that much emotional pain? Yet, there was something in me that knew I was right where I was meant to be; for the first time in my whole life I was good at something, and that something made me feel I was a part of the human race. At last I had a sense of worthiness, at last I understood why I had never before felt I belonged. Suddenly, all of my past and my life so far made sense. Mediumship is a piece of the puzzle that is my life, which made the whole mishmash look like an actual picture.

There came a time when I was booked to lead a Sunday service at a local church. This generally involves saying an opening prayer and reading from a book of my choice, one that I hope will be of comfort to those listening. Following that comes an address where I speak for twenty minutes on the philosophy of spiritualism and the afterlife, or some other topic I think is profound and will uplift the congregation. The last part of the service is a demonstration of mediumship. This was my first time actually leading and I was so nervous, I thought, "Somebody please just break my arm so I do not have to do this service."

As I sat at home, waiting until it was time to head to the church, I noticed I had a little alcohol left over from my Saturday night with friends. It was vodka. I didn't have any mixer left, but that didn't matter. I thought, "Well, people who have something nerve wracking to attend to, often have a little "Dutch courage," and I proceeded, in my desperate state, to take a sip or two of the vodka. A few minutes later, a friend of mine drove me to the church. I remember thinking, "Maybe I shouldn't have had the vodka."

A few minutes later, there I was on the platform in front of the entire congregation. Only I was completely worse for wear from the vodka. I felt drunk! Oh my God, what was I going to do? I heard the chairperson introduce me and thought, "I can't speak! And how on Earth am I going to stand?" Then I said a quick prayer: "Spirit please help me. I am so sorry."

Then, in what seemed like the background, I heard someone say, "Please welcome Deborah to our platform."

Panicked, I stood up and walked to the front and... I was completely sober! All traces of the alcohol had gone. I could not believe it. I was so thankful to my guides; they had taken away the drunken feeling to allow me to be able to work. At the end of the service I thanked my guides over and over again, and I promised them that I would never drink alcohol and work ever. To this day, I have kept that promise.

I wanted to share that story with you, one, to put you off ever being tempted to drink before working. But mainly I wanted to make clear just how nervous we can be and how much that nervousness can affect us. If ever you feel like you are too anxious to be a medium, and feel like giving up, please remember that I have been through the same thing to a massive degree and I lived to tell the tale. There is good news in this: things do get much better and easier the longer you work. Today, I do not get nervous at all. I may get butterflies just before demonstrating, but only to what would be considered a normal degree. I no longer feel any of the terrible anxiety that used to plague me.

I have now been working as a medium, teaching, demonstrating and conducting one to one private readings in the UK, USA, Canada and Europe for the last eight years. If I can do it, so can you.

My husband Paul and I founded The Accolade Academy of Psychic and Mediumistic Studies in 2008. The rest, dear reader, is, as they say, history.

Chapter 11

How to Deal with Nerves in Your Work

In the high country of the mind one has to become adjusted to the thinner air of uncertainty...

Robert M. Pirsig

Many globally known mediums and psychics often give excuses to explain the poor quality of their work, failing to acknowledge that nerves play a huge part in their failure to perform. I often tell students in our workshops that the very most we can expect to get out of them on any given workshop day is about sixty percent. The other forty percent is lost, as tension tends to stunt sensitivity. Because let's face it, regardless of our surroundings, the minute we let our nerves overcome us we slip into familiarity, relying on confident past experiences as a safety net. You see, nerves are the result of the self-doubts we place on ourselves. And these doubts come from the fear that we might make a mistake or be seen as a non-achiever in front of others, either in class or whilst working professionally with our mediumship.

The resulting nerves can derail any career, simply from the message your lack of confidence advertises to others. Our nerves and ego are always at war with each other. When our ego is threatened, often all we want is to escape whatever situation has created the threat. Within the realms of mediumship, such situations would exist in most working environments, such as one to one reading appointments and public demonstrating.

We all have a panic button that lives deep inside our ego. Before I learnt to understand my nerves, I could get myself in a hell of a mess during audience demonstrations. The thought of being wrong while giving evidence was so overwhelming I'd panic. My nerves would kick in and Bang! I would immediately look for something familiar to get me through. Of course, this never worked. As my nerves sucked my confidence, I dug myself into a deeper and deeper mess with my evidence.

And I wasn't the only one. Anxiety would see my Debs unable to eat for up to twelve hours before any live show. The journeys to shows with the two of us nervous together were sometimes tense to say the least. Being a working couple, we had to get to grips with the situation very early, not only for our careers but also for the sake of our relationship. As with any issue, the place to start is with you.

As training/working mediums or psychics we need to learn to understand our nerves, become friends with them and recognize why they feel so monstrous the second we allow them to dive in. Yes, that's correct - when we allow.

Being judged by others is a biggy in this industry, so it is important to train yourself to hold a sense of self-praise in your work, whilst also becoming a little thick-skinned as they say. Truth being, the more efficient you become in your work, the more criticism you will receive from clients and fellow mediums. You will fare better if you raise your tolerance to this kind of let down from the onset. It is also important to understand that the start of any live show or one to one reading will be tense. Making that first link to someone in the audience is like stepping into the unknown. It does get easier, however, and what makes it easier is you - the self-belief you grow in nurturing the thought that you can do this job. You don't have to be a seasoned worker, just create the thought that makes the belief that makes the action. It's universal law - you can't go wrong.

When nerves do strike, remember that you are participating in something you love. Mediumship came to you freely. It was your choice to use and develop your talents, so it's very personal to you. For this reason, when your mediumship does not follow plan, your over-exaggerated ego will want to kick in. You'll feel like you are letting your client or audience down. That's when you panic - nerves pile on and wham! There you have it, full circle. When that happens, tell yourself that your nerves are simply a reminder of the love and care you have for what it is you are doing with your mediumship. It is up to you to use the energy that nerves provide as a positive, to accept them as a subtle reminder that they are there to help you sustain the quality of your work.

I've given my nerves a name. This sounds crazy, I know, but it works for me. By giving them a name, I've made my nerves individual, made a friend out of them, a guardian almost. When I feel them kicking in, I tell myself a friend is there, reminding me that I care as much about my mediumship now as ever. If they show signs of popping up when I'm in the middle of a live show, I know my nerves are just reminding me that I need to be a little stronger, to believe in myself and work through the moment. I love my nerves and know they love me. Learn to love yours. They are there because they love you.

Chapter 12
The Father Who Once Was

Synchronicity reveals the meaningful connections between the subjective and objective world.

Carl G. Jung

All careers have moments of synchron-icity that in one way or another are memory milestones, moments when you scratch your head in wonder and think to yourself: "I never expected this to happen." This chapter relates one of my biggest memory milestones yet.

In August 2010, Debs and I were demonstrating our mediumship in a bar deep in the Welsh valleys. It was not the biggest place in the world, with so many people pushed in that we had very little room to work. This was one of those evenings I told you about when my nerves were jumping in my tummy and I was fighting to stay in control. This was your typical Welsh audience - a mid-week night out, with booze and I remember thinking, "Damn it's going to get very loud in here once the alcohol kicks in."

Getting started, Debs and I went through our typical introduction. I started with the first link, approaching what I thought looked like two sisters in the audience. I was incorrect, as you will see. (Serves me right, for letting my

71

mind come in and make a judgment.) I proceeded to give evidence of what I felt was one of the lady's brothers in spirit, which she said was correct. Right off, the spirit contact gave his name and details of his personality. I found the spirit contact very easy and in some ways uplifting to work with. It was a link I enjoyed, which calmed my nerves and helped me start with confidence.

The evening proceeded without incident. Then, during our halftime break, as Debs and I went outside to get some fresh air, the two ladies from the start of the demonstration followed us. Generally in such situations, we try to avoid any discussion with audience members, as that might be seen as fishing for information. Soon the younger of the two, who I had given the message to earlier, came over and asked, "Do you know who I am?" My first thought was, here we go, some medium wanting to flex her ego. I politely said, "Sorry but I don't remember you. Have we met?" "Yes," she said. "You were a young boy then, so you may not remember me. I am your Aunty."

My stomach fell to the floor. My Mother was married before she met the man I call my Dad, the Dad who made me his own. I was only eighteen months old when he rescued my Mother from a life of single parenting, as my blood father had thankfully run off with my Mother's best friend after putting my Mam through many years of abuse.

With my heart racing, I quietly repeated the word "Aunty."

"Yes," she said. "From your mother's first marriage."

I advised her I did not know any of my relatives relating to that time, as I chose not to keep in touch out of loyalty to my dad of now. I went on to explain that her brother, my blood father, must be a man of no morals to beat a woman the way he did my Mother, and that I had no interest in knowing anything about him. She said totally she understood why I felt this way, as she was aware of the way he had treated my Mother all those years ago. Then she patiently asked that I hear her out.

She proceeded to explain that there was another side to her brother that was good and although there was no excuse for his actions he had also been abused as a child along with all of the other children in their family. I still found it hard to be sympathetic and felt loyalty to my mother rebelling in my tummy even as she delivered this bombshell:

"You were just linking with your dad from spirit," she said. "The brother you gave me from spirit was your father."

The words OH MY GOD rushed through my thoughts. How, I wondered, could I not feel that? This man did not feel like the shit of a man who beat my Mam. Truthfully, he felt quite nice, telling his sister how much he loved her and remembering how they had had to be strong together during their childhood. I mean, he even went on to talk about how he'd tried to protect her from the hurt they had to encounter.

So, why did I not feel the usual sense of recognition I get when linking with my family in spirit? I often feel my Grandmother and other relatives who have passed, and they are all familiar. Surely as this was my blood Dad I should have received some sign.

In thinking this over, I've concluded that maybe I encountered him that way so I could experience his gentler side without the distraction of memory. Would I have maintained the link if I had known who he was? That's questionable. But is it my right to make such judgments? After all, our blueprint is there for the evolvement of all involved. My Aunt informed me my blood Father ended by taking his own life, which for me speaks to what he must have gone through during his time here. Can I justify his actions now, knowing what his life was like? That's a hard one for me. If I cannot forgive him, then I have to wonder if I am as spiritual as I claim to be. But if I do forgive him for his actions, am I then saying it was okay for him to beat my Mother?

I remember going for a one to one reading whilst at Stansted College in England, and being told by the medium that a dad was there for me in spirit and that he spent many hours while in my village watching us, his children, playing through the school gates. My thoughts then were, "No way, not him, not the dad we have been told about. He was a man of no morals, why would he care about his children?"

Ever since that meeting with my Auntie, I have been working hard to see the bigger picture in regard to people's actions in life, particularly towards those they claim they love. I really thought that if I ever encountered my blood dad from spirit I would experience the side of him my mother experienced, the side of him we were told about countless times. I never expected the loving feeling I experienced from him on that night.

Holding resentment for a father I never met all these years was a piece of cake up to that evening. Truthfully I never expected to meet my blood Father during my life here. For me meeting John Boswell was a life changing moment, one that released a battle of emotions and a tug of war of loyalties I never expected. If I deny what I felt that evening, then I have very little trust in my work and my loyalty to my mediumship is for nothing, if I trust what I felt then John Boswell was capable of being a loving man.

As the months passed after that event, and as my thoughts evolved, I became more and more curious about John. Occasionally, I feel him close to me from spirit, having that same sense of love I felt that evening, which over time has become just like the familiar spiritual-family feel I spoke about earlier. Am I happy with the contacts I have from John? That would have to be a yes. Does he feel like a dad when we make contact? Truthfully he does in a spiritual sense. Nothing can replace the love I have for my dad here in this life, and what John and my Mother suffered together I cannot change or make better. What I know for sure is that my mother has had a good life with our saviour dad and, for her, those early days are a distant memory that she keeps locked well away.

I feel blessed that I have the belief that enables me to share with John our spiritual reunions together, and over time I've grown enough, emotionally and spiritually, to say I now have two Dads in my life.

Chapter 13
Ghosts

I think that souls agree to come in and do what they're going to do and then leave when they're going to leave. So there's nothing tragic when a soul leaves. I think it was already preordained.

Sally Kirkland

Whoever heard of a place haunted by a noble deed, or of beautiful and lovely ghosts revisiting the glimpses of the moon? Algernon H. Blackwood

Ghosts. I may be the only person in the world who has the following theory on who or what ghosts are; yet I cannot change now, as that would mean lying to myself and that I will not do.

Let us begin with an obvious question: what is a ghost?

According to the Cambridge online dictionary, a ghost is "The spirit of a dead person, sometimes represented as a pale, almost transparent image of that person, which some people believe appears to people who are alive." The Farlex online dictionary defines a ghost as "The spirit of a dead person, especially one believed to appear in bodily likeness to living persons or to haunt former habitats."

From this, we can conclude that ghosts are the spirits of dead people who frequent their former habitats and show themselves to the living in a transparent form of their earthly bodies.

These are of course very weak definitions, particularly as neither gives any explanation at all as to why ghosts would want to hang around and show themselves to people who are "alive."

As I state in other chapters of this book, I fully believe in reincarnation. I also believe that souls must get to a certain point in their evolution before they can be deemed worthy of incarnating in the first place. Now this does not mean we must be perfect or even close to it - but certainly a few steps up from a wild creature. In my view of reincarnation, I feel we are born again as souls far away from light, love and God, with a mission to grow and keep growing for however long it takes us to evolve, at our own pace, until we literally become one again with the undiluted source that we call God.

What about souls who get "stuck" here on Earth? I start with this because a common theory behind all ghosts is that they have for one reason or another gotten themselves trapped on Earth by some sort of self-imprisonment, not knowing about or perhaps not wanting to move towards the light and thus return to their spiritual home. Some people say that ghosts stay here to complete unfinished business and that, over time, they forget how to go back. This is difficult for me to believe for many reasons. Most importantly, a spirit who has worked out his/her life plan with his/her soul group (which I discuss at length in the next chapter), including the exact time of departure from this life, would absolutely NOT have any unfinished business here on Earth.

There is another theory that ghosts remain here because of the "shock" at how quickly they were "thrown" from their bodies. This is no easier for me to accept, as I believe we choose our departure. My belief is there are no accidents in life; our arrival and departure dates are all in conjunction with others in our soul group. One cannot skip out early. As we are all intricately entwined, to do so would interfere with the plans of others.

Furthermore, I feel there are earthly terms and spiritual terms. Say someone dies due to an accident. In earthly terms, if we studied all of the facts it might look as though that person could have somehow avoided the accident. We could say the same for people that commit suicide - if only someone had been with them, if someone had stayed the night or known what they were thinking, the suicide might have been prevented. For people who have an illness and pass over, we could say death might have been prevented if only the illness had been caught it in time, etcetera, and etcetera.

If we look at the same situations in spiritual terms, however, we understand that when we pass over to spirit on a particular day and in a particular way, everything is in perfect order. There is no chaos when it comes to the spiritual side of life. Nothing is random, yet all is freedom.

It is said that we have a free will, that God granted us this wonderful gift. By spiritual law, we always exert the right to our free will, and that can never be interfered with. If we know this to be true, then we understand that to pass over from an accident, in the blink of an eye without any warning to our spirit or without our having chosen it, would be a MASSIVE violation of our free will, would it not? Following this, I believe we choose our departure at some point. If not right at the time of death, the only other time we could make this choice would be before we incarnate. Even this, to my mind, is an act of free will.

We can go a little deeper here and discuss another subject pertaining to spiritual terms: time. There is no time in the realm of the absolute, all happens in the moment of now. Whether this is absolute truth or not (and I believe it is), has little matter for this discussion. For as long as we choose to pass over at some point in time, then our free will be exercised.

If we agree, then, that spirits must have chosen to pass in a particular way and on a particular day, how in the world could one have unfinished business or be so "shocked" at the passing that he/she would not be ready to leave the Earth. Perhaps he/she doesn't know he/she has passed at all and so is a ghost - that is another common explanation.

Another explanation I have heard is that spirits can get too attached to their earthly personalities and addictions (alcohol, drugs, etc.) and therefore be reluctant to actually make a complete transition. There is, again, a massive flaw in this theory. If such a person is indeed dead and now exists as the spirit of that person, then the personality and any addictions connected with his/her physical body would surely have been dropped with the body at the time of passing, leaving nothing to cling to. People would have us believe that our spirits, our intelligent spirits that know their personal plan for eternity and that may have incarnated a few hundred times before, might still crave a human personality over its own wonderful being and progression upwards. Let me tell you that our souls are programmed one way and that is towards evolution! Not towards devolution. We don't find ourselves slipping down the evolutionary scale with pride. We don't find ourselves aiming to come into our next life as a frog or a bee, now do we? No, the nature of spirit is to advance, making it impossible for one to become stagnant. Our earthly personalities understand this simplistic plan of advancement, so why, with the wider angle of vision that our spirit is blessed with, would one choose to stay within the circumstances of the life just lived?

My belief is that spiritual amnesia is a requirement in order for the game of human life to work. This amnesia is only necessary, however, whilst in the physical body and therefore is naturally discarded at the time of passing along with all the other physical tools needed for a physical life.

One might argue that if we as spirits are loving and kind and peaceful there should be no need to incarnate into a physical body in which we then learn to become aspects of God. My answer to this is that it would be much easier to be an aspect of God in a safe, familiar home filled with love, and so we must incarnate in order to be challenged and thus grow. Not that I am suggesting that our spirits are perfect, if that were true there would be no need to incarnate in the first place. Rather, I believe that our spirits are more advanced than the human personality we take on for our earthly tasks. To what degree I couldn't begin to know, yet I know that a life in the body presents us with so much more opportunity for evolvement than that of the spiritual realms, due to the hardships that we endure physically, emotionally, and mentally. And not only are the hardships important, but also the ways in which we overcome such hardships in order to help others, to be of service to our fellow man in spite of those hardships.

The purpose of incarnating is to let our spirit overshadow the personality and work through it to reach a higher state of being. The dream incarnation would be to let our spirit-self be fully realized whilst in the body - that is the goal, to be our real selves whilst on Earth. The more we succeed in this endeavour, the more we heed the words of the greatest medium who ever lived. Our Jesus Christ said we must live "On Earth as it is in Heaven." Thus, the reason for incarnation is to evolve enough to enable both our being and our planet to become a paradise.

So, to go back to ghosts. Yes, I do believe in ghosts, and yes, I do believe people see and encounter ghosts, as they are a very real part of this life. "Ugh," I hear you say, after all that I have just written! Let me explain: my belief is that, when needed, a spirit will show up in order to be seen, to be acknow-ledged, for the purpose of some greater good. Say there is a ghost hunt in some old, gothic castle somewhere, or that you are a visitor to a public house that is said to be haunted, or to any building with a past. In such circumstances, I believe a "volunteer" will show up, and will continue to show up, on occasion to allow participants or residents to experience something that will make them think, something that will inspire them to explore the possibilities and come to their own truths about the afterlife. There is a much bigger purpose being met than participants could ever imagine, and that goes the same anywhere and anytime there is para-normal activity. I must also mention here that sometimes the only way to make yourself known as an unseen spirit is to move things, throw things, touch people, make footsteps, blow out candles, slam doors, turn lights on and off, etc. It would be no good to exist only to stand still unnoticed.

As for the idea that there are "bad spirits": I cannot believe this, as I feel we can only incarnate on Earth or have access to Earth when our light is bright enough. Again, I am not saying that spirit must emit a big bright, angel-type light, just light enough. Many "bad" people are so called because they have lowered their light just for that lifetime to bring about situations for the purpose of helping to evolve others. Shakespeare said, "All the world's a stage and we but play a part." I believe this is what he was referring to. Also we need to remember that the personality of the human being is dropped when we die, so bad people are not so bad once passed over.

So bad spirits or, as I like to say, baby spirits, due to the love of God and the desire to make the order out of chaos

81

necessary for this life plan to work, are not light enough to come anywhere near Earth. But just for this conversation, let us say they were allowed to come here. We need to bear in mind then that these baby souls have no conscience, they don't feel any remorse and they have no logical thinking or any love in them whatsoever. Not forgetting that they could hurt us or kill us if they wanted, do we then suppose they would come to Earth just to scare us a little? That, though they could really do damage, they decide instead to just play with us - slamming doors, turning off lights, etc. We must be logical when dealing with spiritual matters. If baby spirits could harm us, they would, in which case all of us humans would be dropping like flies. There would be nobody left living on Earth surely.

We must also understand that it would be chaos to have souls of major deferring degrees of evolvement in the same space. As much as we think there is a huge difference between Mother Theresa and a serial killer, we each play a part in the evolvement of others whilst on Earth. In having this discussion, we have to remember that God is the Supreme Being, the undiluted source of pure love, a love and an intelligence that we can never fully comprehend until the time that we are near to being part of that same undiluted source. I have absolute confidence, faith and trust that our God has all of this figured out.

Finally, there are those that believe that we can call on evil spirits, and once called upon those spirits then haunt us! So is it the case that once we call on a spirit we then have a monster running around to contend with? A monster that carries the moral attitude that "Only those who call upon me shall be my victims"? Again I urge you to think logically and not with the childish mind of an eight year old playing with Masters of the Universe figures.

In conclusion, my belief is that our spiritual journey is an inward journey, one that cannot be sustained by any outward source or through second hand stories. YES there are ghosts, but to my mind it is more like a case of ghosts on demand, spirits who are here for a purpose and for the greater good of mankind. They appear to us in order to allow people the experience of encountering paranormal activity, as a means of awakening human minds to the spirit within, for the purpose of evolvement.

Chapter 14
Soul Groups

You are infinite. You are really everywhere. But you think that you are the body, and therefore consider yourself limited. If you think you are the body which is sitting, you do not know your true nature. –

Meher Baba

When first approaching the subject of the afterlife, many people get confused as to the difference between a spirit and a soul. Some people believe that the two are interchangeable and that "soul" is just another name for a "spirit." In reality, a spirit is the individual spiritual being that remains after we pass away and have left our physical body. For instance, my Dad departed this life on a cold Christmas evening in 2001; who and what he is now is a spirit. His spirit, after earthly death, then returned to a group of spirits. This spirit family is called a soul. As mediums, we understand that there are many spirits to a single soul. For clarity, we call this soul a "soul group," because even though the word soul is singular there is more than one spirit within it. This, I believe, is where the confusion lies - in the traditional grammatical definition of soul. Although we can, by this definition, use the words soul, soul group or spiritual family to describe the same thing, for the purposes of this conversation I will refer to them as soul groups.

Now, here is the next concept: soul groups are not all equal. Each group contains spirits who are at the same level of evolvement. These spirits will incarnate together on Earth for the purpose of evolving further and becoming purer degrees of love/God. God and love for me are the same word, so whenever I say God I mean love and whenever I say love I mean God. We all have soul groups to which we belong. These personal groups are made up of the spirits of our mums and dads, brothers, sisters, sons and daughters, friends, partners, and any other person strongly connected to us in this life. They include people who were supportive and loving in this life, as well as those who caused us the most pain. Either way, they help the evolution of our spirits and/or provide opportunities for our growth here on Earth. There will come a time when you and your soul group will have undergone all of the evolvement one can achieve on Earth. At that time, the members of this group will no longer need to incarnate. I do not believe there are spirits living on Earth who have incarnated on their own without being members of a soul group. The only possible exception would be a highly evolved spirit, such as Jesus, here for the huge task of bringing about the spiritual evolution of many.

As for the details and processes of soul groups, I don't believe anyone here on Earth knows the complete answer. We agree to a spiritual amnesia when incarnating, in that we have no memory of our true spiritual home or our true nature as spirits while occupying our earthly minds and bodies. I believe this amnesia is necessary; if we knew with one hundred per cent certainty that we were spirits with a spiritual home that we could go to without first needing to gain the maturity that comes with evolvement, we would have no incentive to remain here on Earth. When the going got tough, most of us would end our earthly life prematurely. The game would be up, so to speak.

Some people think that any belief in an afterlife is wishful thinking. I cannot agree. For me, believing that there is nothing after this existence would be much simpler; it would be a case of, "Oh well, that's that then," without all of the debate and confusion.

Of those who do believe in an afterlife, there are some who claim that we will keep the same personalities after we pass over - that we will remain the same "Deb," "Jayne," or "Paul" that we were whilst here on Earth. They also claim that we have an identical spirit body to match our physical body, which we carry with us after we pass. Basically, this belief says that we are exactly the same when we pass, only without our physical bodies. Hmmmmm... In this same vein, there are countless mediums who, whilst communicating with spirit from the other side, declare, "He/she is fine now!" Meaning, they can walk or they can talk, or they have arms now or they don't have cancer anymore. In other words, they are cured of physical illness, but they are still the same person with the same personality. How could it be that the only change we undergo after passing away is the loss of our physical bodies? If that were so, what in the name of God, literally, would be the point of incarnating in the first place? For us to end up exactly the same, with the same personality and a spirit-body identical to our physical body? I'm sorry, but I absolutely do not agree with that.

Other people think that whatever belief an individual has about heaven, hell, and the afterlife, that is what they will experience when they pass over. That is, they believe the afterlife is subjective to the individual and that heaven is not an automatic one-experience-for-all. For instance, say Fred thinks that Heaven consists of fields and streams and meadows - well, then that is where his spirit will go and what it will experience after death. If Mary thinks, due to the teachings of her religion, that she is not good enough in God's eyes or that she has sinned beyond repair and so will go to a place with fire and brimstone, that is what her spirit will experience. And if John believes that he has to sleep in his grave until "Judgment Day" then his spirit will sleep in his grave until Judgment Day. To anyone who supports this theory, I must ask - Is it in a spirit's nature to sleep? What happens if John is cremated against his wishes? Does his spirit sleep then in his pot of ashes until the day of judgment? I'm serious. Somebody please enlighten me!

Are we to honestly believe this is the process? That God would say to us, "Oh, you are going to be a really brave little spirit and you are going to incarnate into a harsh environment, compared to your spiritual home. In that environment you will often feel alone, because by default you are meant to feel alone, regardless of how much you are loved whilst there on Earth, as this will help with your evolvement. Because you are loved unconditionally whilst in your spiritual residence, it will feel harsh, yet it is a necessary part of the process. You have before you a life that will for the most part be full of lessons designed to help you become, to some degree, your chosen aspect of God. These lessons will not be easy to achieve. You have chosen to acquire patience in order for it to meld into your spirit being. In this way, you will take patience back to your spiritual home where you will keep it for eternity. The only way you can acquire such patience is to have situations come up in your life that enable you to practice. This will be frustrating and it will take a lot of willpower to achieve, particularly given that you have chosen an earthly personality that, due to its childhood has no patience at all. You will also want to take forgiveness back with you in your spirit, and this is another tough one, as you will have to go through many hurtful experiences in order to learn forgiveness, or at least a small aspect of it. You have also signed up to learn about loss in this lifetime, another really tough aspect as you will have to watch as people, processions, and your sense of self, etc. slip away from your life. How fast you learn and then acquire these aspects will be entirely up to you. Because of this, you will have the potential to acquire the three aspects of God in this one lifetime even though most spirits do not pass the grade with even one aspect."

You see, achieving such leaps and bounds in just one lifetime is rare. If you look around at the people in your life, how many can you count who are not bitter about past situations or, even worse, hindered by them? How many have not become hard or closed off? How many are fearful of being vulnerable? How many do you know that are scared of life? Who do you know who substitutes alcohol, drugs, prescription drugs, or cigarettes for real feelings? How many of these few examples can you recognize within yourself?

After being told all of this and after going through all of this, the idea that we might end up back in the spirit world with the same personality and spiritual body seems rather a stupid exercise. Not only stupid, but also pointless and heartbreakingly disappointing. I for one would say to God, "You know what? No thanks. I'd rather stay here in the comfort of my spiritual home." But of course that is not the way it happens, as this would defy all logic. Rather, it is my belief that all of the above is true, at least as regards the sequence of events, yet the out-come is quite different.

Most of the people in your soul group - your family, friends, spouses, lovers and enemies in this life - are the main players in your quest to gain the aspects of God that you will eventually bring back to your spiritual home and soul group. Remembering, of course, when you meet up with them once again, to thank them all (especially your so-called enemies and those who challenged you the most) with much gratitude for presenting you with the situations in your earthly life that allowed you to bring the prize home.

When a medium works and communicates with a loved one from the other side, then they must bring forth the personality of the spirit contact, otherwise how else could the recipient recognize their mother/father/brother/sister, etc.? Now, I am not suggesting that mediums do not describe the contacts' personalities as they were on Earth, of course we do. Otherwise there would be no evidence that the spirit that was once their loved one was there before them. Nor am I suggesting that we won't recognize our loved ones because they have changed so much since they passed. On the contrary, I believe the spirit part of them is much more familiar to us than their earthly personalities ever were. Why, for instance, do many of us still love our parents, children, sisters or brothers even after they do terrible things? I believe it is because we know who they really are; somewhere in the core of us we know the plan and know that this behaviour is part of that plan.

Take my Father for instance. Liam was a very troubled man, and he had good reason to be. Or not, the choice was obviously his. He was born a little baby, a blank page. All was new, just as it is for the rest of us, but circumstances (which I believe he chose before he incarnated, as do we all) led him to be an abused child, abused in all the ways a child can be. That does not a healthy adult make. Dad became a violent alcoholic. Violent to counteract feelings of inadequacy, vulnerability, guilt, self-loathing and disgust, alcoholic in order to escape those very same feelings.

You see, my Dad was a priest in his early life in Ireland, and had been since he was ten years old. He went from living in his childhood home where he was a cherished and loved, blonde haired, blue-eyed boy. The last born of ten children, he had six older sisters and three older brothers, who all adored him. He was sent from that environment into the harsh life of living as a beautiful little boy in the priesthood in Ireland in the 1950s. Say no more.

So Dad was made what he was by his life's circumstances. I'm sure he was not a violent little boy. If my dad then was "turned into" an alcoholic with a violent temper (via circumstances), why in the world would he continue to be an angry, violent spirit when he went back to the spirit world? This was not, after all, who he began as in the first place. The same is true for most of us. Unless we really take note of what is happening to us and work out what aspects we have come to this life to obtain, life - with all of the circumstances of our existence that make us harder, colder, more cautious, bitter, angry, regretful, etc. - can get in the way. By the way, you can determine these aspects by looking at your weakness: what are the problems that keep reoccurring in your life? Do people leave you again and again? Do you find yourself responsible for everybody's feelings or lives? Do you find you are always waiting for things or people to come in your life? Do you value possessions over people? Are you jealous? These are your clues. Once you see them clearly and act on them accordingly, they will disappear. Generally the people that give you the hardest time are those who are closest to you in your soul groups. That is why nine times out of ten it is family that causes you the most heartache and joy - because you have made a pact with them to be who you are, the personality you have adopted for this lifetime, in order for them and for you to grow. My Dad came to chat with my husband Paul a good while after he passed, and mentioned "the evolvement" he had "allowed" me to have. That was a huge statement and a difficult one for me to hear. Had I really looked at it like that until then? The truth is, I had not. Yet that is it right there. Your family, friends, colleagues, spouses, etc., are your greatest teachers.

Please, please remember, we must pay attention to the messages we are teaching and passing on to young mediums coming up. What we say must make sense. I say this because I have met a lot of the people who simply pass along what they have heard from others without giving a thought to whether it makes sense. The truth is, the communicator will always try to get across to their living relatives that they are okay, NOT that they are exactly the same. There is a HUGE difference.

Here is what makes more sense to me. Firstly, as regards reincarnation: there would be no point whatsoever for us to incarnate just once. That would be like God saying, "Oops, there goes your only chance to evolve on Earth." Do you believe God would only let you have a single go at one of the most amazing tools we're given with which to evolve? Even we, mere mortals, give our children mock exams!

Assuming reincarnation is a fact, what happens to "Debs," the personality, when I pass over into the spirit world and discard my body? I cannot still be Debs because I have been many personalities throughout the history of my time - retaining the personality of each life would be impossible. Otherwise I would still be Ugg the caveman/woman surely. Seriously, my belief is that of course we retain the good gained in life, though maybe we can swap the word "good" here with "evolvement," as I believe those two words are, in this respect, interchangeable. And so there will always be a little part of Debs that I carry within my spirit until the time that I become one with the undiluted, pure love that is God. I also believe that we constantly grow in that direction.

My theory, to put it in simple terms, is that the Big Bang was God breathing out, and we will spend the next forever as soul groups returning, evolving at our own pace until we all merge with the one they call God. Ready for a time when the next Big Bang will set us far out again, ready to make that Journey once more....and forever more.

Chapter 15

Do Animals Have a Spirit?

If having a soul means being able to feel love and loyalty and gratitude, then animals are better off than a lot of humans.
James Herriot

"A dog has the soul of a philosopher."
Plato

What an interesting question! I for one hadn't really thought much about the subject until recently. I knew animals were very special and I believed they had the same value as us human beings. Like any other living wonder on this planet, I assumed that after death they went to a heavenly place, and gave it no more attention. My chosen field of study is the journey of human spirits and our ability to reconnect with them after they passed over to their spiritual home. More and more frequently, however, animals, once loved on Earth but now lost to their loving owners, come through to be remembered while I conduct readings. This increase has prompted me to look further into the subject of animal spirits.

In the book *Conversations with God* Neale Donald Walsh asks God, "Do animals have souls?" God answers, "You only have to look into the eyes of an animal to know whether they have a soul or not." I agree. If you look into your loving pet's eyes you'll see all of their feelings. You will know if your loyal companion is happy, sad, lonely, content or comfortable. I feel those of us who share a loving bond with our pets can agree that knowing how he or she feels is naturally clear in our everyday connection with them. Furthermore, I would not restrict our understanding of animal feelings to the suburban household's best friends, but would include wild animals everywhere.

People often use the term "dumb animal." Dictionary.com defines the word dumb as "lacking in intelligence or good judgment; stupid; dull witted, also one lacking the power of speech (often offensive when applied to humans): Dumb Animal."

My belief is that the true meaning of the word "dumb" has been exaggerated to elevate our human race in such a way as to lower the respected equality of the animal kingdom. In its origin, the word "dumb" simply referred to someone (I assume that meant a person, not an animal) who lacked the power of speech. So here's a question - what is speech in its truest sense? If, according to the Wikipedia.com, speech is "the vocalized form of human communication," how can the animal language of communication bear any comparison to the word speech? Are we humans suggesting that any form of life that cannot converse in our chosen form of communication be labelled dumb? If that's the case, I must question the intelligence of my fellow species.

In my opinion I find speech in whatever language we use to be the least reliable form of communication. Let's face it, we are not all as honest as is often claimed, as many people lie about, play down or exaggerate their feelings much of the time. A feeling can tell you so much more than the spoken word ever could. How arrogant of us to think that because animals do not speak words like us, they are less intelligent. These beautiful creations, especially in their wild and natural habitat, show remarkable signs of logical thinking as well as expressing all of the instinctual feelings that one would expect of a human being. They also express feelings of a maternal or paternal nature, such as jealousy, loyalty and playfulness, no different to the most expressive of our kind.

Much like humans, most animals experience very particular feelings and thought patterns. Take for instance, the wise words of Charles Darwin, which I feel sum up the point I am trying to make: "There is no fundamental difference between man and the higher mammals in their mental faculties... The difference in mind between man and the higher animals, great as it is, certainly is one of degree and not of kind. We have seen that the senses and intuitions, the various emotions and faculties, such as love, memory, attention and curiosity, imitation, reason, etc., of which man boasts, may be found in an incipient, or even sometimes a well-developed condition, in the lower animals." A fine example of this is evident in the range of responses displayed when an animal is called upon to defend its pack or young. A mama bear whose cub is threatened grows angry and defensive, reacting in the same way we would whilst protecting our family and home. Similarly, when an animal finds itself in a position of having to choose life or death, having to acknowledge and act upon a feeling that is potentially dangerous to itself in order to save another by choosing courage over fear, this carries the same detail of thought as used by our brave soldiers during conflict. And may I also say there are a lot of the instinctual feelings mentioned above that many of our urban human companions have conveniently lost over time.

It seems that many have come to the belief that no being a fraction of our human size could ever be a match for us intellectually or spiritually. Since when did worthiness of having a spirit and a life after life equate to intelligence or size? Take ants for instance: they have a fantastically complex social structure that implies a logical intelligence when working together for the greater good of the whole nest. This teamwork allows for the protection of each individual ant whilst being more productive for all. It seems to me that the everyday common ant has a more loving connection, with a greater sense of community with its own species than many of us do as humans. Not only do their habits portray intelligence much like our own, it would seem that spiritually they have surpassed some of the human race.

Or let us compare humans to the household cat. Most humans live with feelings of self-consciousness and unworthiness to some degree, and constantly work on themselves to overcome their lack of self-confidence whilst riding a lifelong, emotional rollercoaster of happiness and sadness. At the same time, we strive to make "better" lives for ourselves, working harder and trying to earn more money, rushing here and there, and unnecessarily competing with our neighbour's materialistic possessions and all that is modern in our world. In addition, we constantly worry and fret about future events that probably won't happen, while carrying with us (and complaining about) incidents that occurred some twenty or thirty years ago.

We experience all of this anxiety, and for what? Are we insane? Yes, very likely! We don't see our cats running here and there, worrying all the time, always thinking ahead in order to beat the next cat. No! Now is all that matters to the cat; now lasts forever for the cat. They say cats are the most Zen-like creatures of all the animal kingdom and you can see why. Study your cat for a day and watch how he lives. You may even want to take a leaf out of his book. Although there are exceptions even to that rule! Allow me tell you about my cat Bailey: he was my boy, like a little son to me. He was half Persian - so beautiful, pure white and fluffy. Yet let me tell you - dull as a brush was he! He had no grace as a cat at all. Jumping from the sofa to the windowsill was a classic move of his! He almost always missed or would land awkwardly, legs splaying out all ways. Another personality trait of Bailey was that he was scared of the wind! If I let him outside when it was windy, he would cower down with his ears back and walk as if he was in a hurricane, dramatic and in slow motion. Yes, scared of his own shadow was our Bail. He couldn't catch a cold let alone a bird or mouse. (Bailey never caught a thing in his life, which was perfect for me.) There was nothing Zen-like about Bailey. Yet to me that just made him all the more loveable. I tell this story of my Bailey to say that any being that displays individuality of any kind (which is any living thing) must have a spiritual self.

It is my belief that all living things on this Earth, including flowers, grass, trees and plants, have their equivalent spirit that reappears in the spiritual realm - just as we do.

I have heard that each animal has a soul group, which is, a group that our furry little friends belong to when they go back to their spiritual home and gather together - cats together, dogs together, birds together, etc. It has also been said that animals that have passed on before us will come to us when we go home to spirit, and stay until you both feel it is time for them to go back to their own soul group. How true this is I cannot tell you. Whenever I am grappling with such an issue, however, I respond with the following: whatever the question, think of the most loving answer. For our loving little companions to spend time with us once we return to our spiritual home makes sense, as that is a loving answer to the question of whether we see our animals once we pass over. It is my belief that when the human species reaches a certain level of awareness and trades the need to eat meat for a vegetarian diet, so will all creatures in the animal kingdom stop eating one another. As we evolve as human beings, the whole planet evolves with us. I believe this is what was meant when Jesus said, "And the lion shall lay down with the lamb." All creatures have a spirit, we all come from one God, and one of God's favourite words is "unity." We are all one.

Many times, too many to count, I have had clients' beloved animals come through in readings to let their owners know they are all right. This delights my clients as much as hearing from a close relative, sometimes more so. Not only do the animals wish to reassure just as a human would, but they also communicate exactly the same way humans communicate. I get the same feelings and thoughts from dogs, cats and rabbits, etc., as I do from Auntie Mary and Uncle Fred. And I would bet my bottom dollar that my story of beautiful Bailey is one of millions around the world of people falling in love with their pets, each with their own, different, wonderful personalities that make us love and cherish them. Animals are without a doubt as individual as us humans.

And so, to the question, do animals have spirits, I say without question, without a doubt in my mind, an absolute resounding YES! Animals do have spirits. Do they communicate with mediums just as our other relatives do? Another absolute yes. Being the recipient and the giver of their messages, and having one hundred per cent trust in a God of love, I am completely confident in my findings. And will Rover, Tiddles, Harry the hamster, Bob the budgie and Bailey the beautiful cat, be there to meet us when it is our time to venture back to our spiritual home? You can bet your life they will.

Chapter 16
Stress-Free Mediumship: The Format

Before anything else, preparation is the key to success.
Alexander Graham Bell

As I see it, spiritualism has gotten bogged down with spiritualism. Too many practitioners place all of the their power as mediums on the shoulders of the spirit world, claiming that the content, clarity, and accuracy of their evidence is completely governed and controlled by those from spirit. This is a typical buck-passing excuse many mediums use for being unable to deliver finer details, such as names of loved ones passed and dates of important events. We only have so much time with any one audience, and in that time it's our job to provide as much evidence with as many links as possible. The key, and the difficulty, comes in remaining calm despite the pressure this knowledge creates. When I first began participating in demonstrations, I found myself quite nervous, with upset stomach and anxiety over how I would perform. I knew if I was to continue, and ever be effective, I would have to find some way to make the process less complicated and therefore less daunting.

In such situations, I found myself asking, "Where do I come in? Must I always put myself in such a nerve-wracked condition simply because I am unsure of the way I will begin?"

It got so bad, I was practically praying for that first link to be good to me. Then I thought, NO WAY! After all, why should anyone waste all that great energy on being nervous rather than working? I'm convinced our spiritual helpers want our time to be as stress-free as possible. As I said, our job is to make links, give evidence and move on to the next person. One way to accomplish this is by looking for a familiar feeling or a prompt of some kind to know when it is time to move on. I can't tell you the number of times I've watched mediums stand in front of an audience and almost plead with spirit for a message to share, or how many times I have seen a medium/psychic start with a piece of evidence that is so random and vague that any confidence they hoped to build with their audience is lost before they begin.

We all need schedules, procedures and rules to maintain structure and help promote a higher quality of life. Mediumship is no different. After all, this is a job and all jobs have rules and procedures. When I'm giving evidence, it is my job not spirit's to decide how I want to start and in what order I want to pass on my evidence. Looking at it a little closer, I realized that I could give any detail of evidence I wished. It was my responsibility to decide for myself what opening line would make my link to the recipient as easy and as absolute as possible for me while also guaranteeing the credibility of my opening piece of evidence. That was my great moment of understanding. Oh my god, I thought, how easy is that? Mediums have been putting all the responsibility on spirit, claiming spirit will provide whatever is needed at the time. And while, yes, this has to be true, we must remember that we are the technicians, ours are the minds that are present and working. We are not locked in a trance or in any way overpowered and so cannot be influenced or lose control of the words that come from our mouths.

From that time on, I introduced what I call the "format" into my work. This technique allows enough space and personal responsibility for a thought without a thought to create happenings in my work. Think of this as you would driving - you know you are in control of the car, and so also know when to check you mirrors, indicate, brake, accelerate and everything else that goes with operating a vehicle. Most of these actions are done without conscious thought. It's like having years of experience on a particular subject or job - this experience may make it so that eighty percent of the time you spend discussing your subject is on autopilot. You can aid this process by organizing your thoughts within your area of expertise. It's like having a mental filling cabinet in which to store a set schedule of discussion points, removing the need to continually pause and think about your next sentence. That is the basis of your format, working without thinking and still having the thought. HOW GREAT!

In designing this format, my aim was to bring in a tool that could be an evolving, adaptable process while still retaining some elements of permanence. First, I thought about how I wanted to begin my demonstrations. Did I wish to go directly to a recipient in the audience, or did I wish to simply throw a link out to the whole of the audience, waiting for their reaction before narrowing my choice to one recipient. For me, the direct approach is much less stressful, but still produces a greater reaction. This in turn grows the confidence I need from the audience almost instantaneously.

Second, I thought about what I would want to hear from a working medium giving me a message. Right away I would want to know the relationship of the contact the medium claimed to have linked with. After all, I'm sure if my Dad was to link with a working medium, he would want me to be able to recognize his presence as quickly as possible. Then, I would want major details, like how he passed, what the cause was, what his personality was like, what were his memories and hobbies, and what he did for a living.

In devising a format of your own, it can be helpful to place your ideas/goals into a few precise bullet points. Here is an example:

1. I am a direct medium

2. The strongest way to start a link is by knowing the relationship (mam, dad, uncle, auntie, etc.) of my spirit contact to my client. I insist on starting this way and will have this information from spirit at the same point of opening a link with my recipient.

3. How did my contact pass over (illness, etc.)?

4. What were my contact's personality traits - positive and negative?

5. What did my contact do for a living?

6. What memories would my contact share with the recipient?

7. What names would my contact share with the recipient? Why?

8. What place and street names would be remembered?

9. What pets and pet names would the contact share with the recipient?

These are just a few of the items in my format. I always add to my list, as this keeps the development and quality of my mediumship active and current. This format is my contract to spirit, instructing them as to how I wish to receive information. Some bullet points are permanent, as I always need them as I begin with a link. For instance, I always start with the relationship of my contact to the recipient because I like to be direct and because I figure in real life we want to know who it is we are talking to (on the phone, etc.). Introducing one's name or working title to another allows for ease in discussion. If Mam, Dad or any other member from spirit wants to communicate with a loved one, then common sense says they would introduce who they are, or at the very least offer a relationship to allow for instant recognition. From there, I ask for a list of specific details. Your list, of course, might be different. The important thing is to have a format to which you can add, or subtract, details.

Remember, the format is your contract to spirit; you decide what works best for you. Your guides and loved ones passed will always want to receive the maximum benefit from any given opportunity each time you work. They always want what is best for you, but it's up to you to determine how stress-free you wish to make your mediumship. Use the format as the foundation of your mediumship. It's not something you need know in absolute order; once written, you've sent its content to the universe, and your guides will take note. When first writing my format, I had a sense of YES, AT LAST! from my guides, and from that day onwards I have never gone blank. And be assured, this format has already proven itself through thousands of Accolade students. This wonderful tool will always keep you from getting stuck in your mediumship; use it with the ease it's meant to provide and it will never let you down.

The thing to remember here is all information is spontaneous, just the chapter headings, the bullet point are pre set by you. Spirit just knows what kind of evidence ou are looking for and not th information itself.

Chapter 17
My Format

Remember, your format is a growing process. Keeping it fresh will help you maintain a healthy mediumship. Use this space to start your own format.

Steps for Building My Format, 1st Month:

1.

2.

3.

4.

5.

6.

7.

8.
9.

10.

Steps for Building My Format, 3rd Month:

1.

2.

3.

4.

5.

6.

7.

8.

9.

10.

Steps for Building My Format, 5th Month:

1.

2.

3.

4.

5.

6.

7.

8.

9.

10.

Steps for Building My Format, 7th Month:

1.

2.

3.

4.

5.

6.

7.

8.

9.

10.

Steps for Building My Format, 9th Month:

1.

2.

3.

4.

5.

6.

7.

8.

9.

10.

Steps for Building My Format, 11th Month:

1.

2.

3.

4.

5.

6.

7.

8.

9.

10.

Chapter 18

Conducting Professional One to One Readings

Strive not to be a success, but rather to be of value
Albert Einstein

As we've discussed, mediumship can be a very stressful career. In my early days, I used to get terribly anxious, particularly before one on one appointments. Boy it was hard. I reckon I must have burnt thousands of calories on nerves alone, and I often caught myself complaining to myself, "Paul, there must be less stressful jobs out there. This is just too much."

So, as I usually do in such situations, I looked to my practical side. To analyze the whole process of conducting one to one appointments before nerves sent me crazy. I broke the appointment procedure down into three stages: before, start/during, and after. The following is what I came up with. It works for me! It could work for you too.

Before

I named this segment of the process "Pleading with Spirit Time." The run up to appointments was an emotional rollercoaster, the worst part being that I never knew if or how spirit would appear. I found myself repeating the phrase "Please be there spirit," almost as often as I was taking potty breaks. This opening prayer was a pitiful sign of my lack of self-worth; soon, I was counteracting such negativity with exaggerated declarations of thankfulness to my guides for being there, even though the appointment had not yet started! What a state of affairs - I was knackered before I'd even begun. The key, I discovered, was in acceptance. I simply could not afford to worry about what might or might not occur during appointments. Think about it; what's the worst than can happen? The client says "no" to some of our evidence, and we have to work a little harder. How bad is that?

Start/During

First, always know that if you have made an appointment, spirit will be there. My motto is, if I turn up for work then work turns up for me. Your intentions are good otherwise you would not put yourself in such a position in the first place. Good intentions = good results ALWAYS. Truth being, if I thought I was going to be let down by my recipients' contacts from spirit each time I showed up for work, then I would get another job. I deserve the same respect that I give to my guides, my mediumship, and those I hold contact with from spirit whilst delivering their message to the recipient. You have to trust your guides and spirit as much as you trust your own desire to go through with the appointment.

Second, refuse yourself the temptation of making any kind of spiritual link or trying to obtain any evidence before the client is sitting right in front of you. Gathering evidence before you're ready to begin can become a habit that creates a breakdown in your flow right from the start. Say you have a thought that you feel is your start. If you have time before the appointment, even if it's just a few minutes, your mind will kick in and expand those thoughts into something they were never meant to be. If you're tempted anyway, ask yourself:

why would the spirit contact have any interest in making contact before the recipient was there to take the communication? And anyway, do you think your guides really want you to work any longer than you have to? Readings are exhausting enough, let alone putting in overtime. You don't start until you start. Be disciplined.

Third, whenever possible always try to start the appointment with evidence of the relationship of the contact from spirit to the client. This is the surest way to instill client confidence in your work. Having this relationship clear also brings a homely comfort to the client, as it lets them know someone they love is there for them. This in turn allows them to relax quickly and be less guarded during the reading. There will be times when you have a clients who has no wish to make contact, or does not want any kind of evidence of loved ones passed. When this happens, relax and go with the flow. Always remember your priorities: medium first, spiritual counsellor second. The more clarity of evidence you deliver to a client from your spirit contact, the stronger the message portion of the appointment will be.

Fourth, keep your personal feelings out of all readings. It's spirit to client, not you to client. Nor should you ever try to make practical sense of your evidence. What I mean is, occasionally a piece of evidence might feel very different to you on a personal level than it does to the client. This does not mean it isn't accurate. Thoughts are presented by spirit that touch a chord within you. You then put those thoughts into words and offer them as evidence. This evidence is then understood and agreed to by your client, who recognizes the words spoken as a match to an issue that resonates with him/her in current life situations. What you must remember is that it's not only important how the evidence is given, but also how it is accepted. For example, you may deliver words of disloyalty to broadly describe a situation relating to your client. In order to give those words, spirit impresses in your thoughts or feelings a time of deceit in your own life, let's say in a relationship. The details of the deceit aren't given, however, and in actuality, it involves the client's work, not a relationship. Now, if you let your personal feelings take over, you might be tempted to go a step further and tell your client the message concerns deceit in a relationship, to which you will receive a "no." Over time you will recognize the process of delivering evidence from spirit to your client, just keep practicing and it will become very obvious to you.

Finally, do not give too much thought to your surroundings while giving a reading, as this is another confidence killer. I have heard many mediums say that they are unable to work if their guides or perhaps one thousand angels have not blessed the reading room. Others insist on the room being in a state of absolute cleanliness with a heavenly energy. The old favourite, however, seems to be the need for candles burning on every available space. The list of demands goes on and on and on. There is no hard or fast rule to remember here. If you are reading in a client's home, you go to your allocated room and do your one to one readings. Why fuss? Remember the lesson from Chapter 5; you can do your job no matter the situation.

Debs and I have held appointments in all kinds of surroundings and locations; it makes no difference where you are working, YOU WORK. Truth being, people are people, venues are venues, countries are countries. You're a medium there to do a job, and yes, we all have our own needs and tastes but that is personal and has nothing to do with your mediumship or your ability to work. As with your personal feelings, keep them separate.

You have to be flexible and courageous in this line of work. See every challenge as a plus in your spiritual toughening and personal development and you'll do a grand job.

After

If it's been a good day, go home, put your feet up and have a glass of wine or cup of coffee or whatever it is you like to do when you relax. Don't give the day's activities anymore thought. You will never bring anything or any spirit home with you, as I'm sure they have better things to do other than hang with a medium all evening. If some of your readings were emotionally challenging and you're still feeling the tail end of that, try to take your thoughts elsewhere. Let it go, just as you would move on from any other matter in life. Again, be disciplined. Work is work and your life is your life. They say mediumship is a way of life and that is correct, but it's not all of your life.

If you have had a really hard day and not all of the readings went according to plan, then it is important to look at what you might have done to correct the situation. Swallow your pride and be truthful to yourself. Perhaps you missed a subtle piece of evidence, or did not share a piece of evidence you received, something ever so small that would have made a difference. Don't look to the client to place blame, as this will weaken both your confidence and your mediumship.

If you follow these basic rules you will do well and I have no doubt become a medium we can all be proud of.

Good luck!

Chapter 19

My One to One Readings

It is important to track your progress in all areas of your mediumship, including your one to one readings. If you are using this book in conjunction with an Accolade Development Plan, you will need to complete 75 One to One readings over the course of two years. If you are using this book for individual study, this number may be different. Either way, please copy the following worksheets as needed. If you need assistance assessing your development, the following questions can be helpful. Always be truthful when answering.

• Could I have done better? Why? Why not?

• Did I work completely from the heart, or did I let my ego take over at any point.

• Was there a time when my thoughts intruded on the reading and blocked the spiritual flow?

• Was the reading repetitive in any way? Did I rely on old evidence at any point in the reading?

Use this space to record and analyze your one to one readings:

Date of Appointment:

Self-Assessment:

Negative Feedback:
Use this section to record any negative feedback you may have received from your client. Then analyze these responses, always looking to yourself first to determine what actions might help you achieve more positive results.

Positive Feedback:
This is your place to feel good! Record any positive feedback received, as it is important to maintaining your momentum, staying focused, and promoting good morale.

Date of Appointment:

Self-Assessment:

Negative Feedback:
Use this section to record any negative feedback you may have received from your client. Then analyze these responses, always looking to yourself first to determine what actions might help you achieve more positive results.

Positive Feedback:
This is your place to feel good! Record any positive feedback received, as it is important to maintaining your momentum, staying focused, and promoting good morale.

Date of Appointment:

Self-Assessment:

Negative Feedback:
Use this section to record any negative feedback you may have received from your client. Then analyze these responses, always looking to yourself first to determine what actions might help you achieve more positive results.

Positive Feedback:
This is your place to feel good! Record any positive feedback received, as it is important to maintaining your momentum, staying focused, and promoting good morale.

Date of Appointment:

Self-Assessment:

Negative Feedback:
Use this section to record any negative feedback you may have received from your client. Then analyze these responses, always looking to yourself first to determine what actions might help you achieve more positive results.

Positive Feedback:
This is your place to feel good! Record any positive feedback received, as it is important to maintaining your momentum, staying focused, and promoting good morale.

Date of Appointment:

Self-Assessment:

Negative Feedback:
Use this section to record any negative feedback you may have received from your client. Then analyze these responses, always looking to yourself first to determine what actions might help you achieve more positive results.

Positive Feedback:
This is your place to feel good! Record any positive feedback received, as it is important to maintaining your momentum, staying focused, and promoting good morale.

Chapter 20
Spirit and Clarity in the English Language

Egotism is the anaesthetic that dulls the pain of stupidity.
                                                    Frank Leahy

Why do some mediums feel it necessary to explain meaningful evidence with words they would never use in everyday life? Correct me if I'm wrong, but do we not claim to be able to link to our loved ones in spirit and pass on messages and evidence that allows the recipient to believe that we, as mediums, have an ability, and their loved ones are truly communicating with us? So why do mediums, many with international experience and recognition in their field, use vague or difficult to understand language to describe evidence and verify their contact from spirit? A classic example of this (and one I often hear) is the mediums who use a single initial in place of the alleged contact's name - whether christian, middle or surname. Let's face it, if you arrange to meet a friend, you do not refer to that person as "the P name." I cannot recall a single time in my life that I ever called anybody by his or her first initial, unless of course I was using a nickname. In doing so, are such mediums claiming that our dear loved ones in spirit have some kind of memory loss or are otherwise no longer able to communicate their complete name? That's just crazy. I'm sure my grandmother remembers my name in its full, as she used it enough. LOL!

When students give evidence during courses at Accolade, we always insist on detailed evidence, telling them it is important to "Start as you mean to go on." And this doesn't just apply to names. If a student says they feel contact from a spirit who loved sport, for instance, then we tell them to say what kind of sport. The same is true for any given subject being discussed by the spirit contact - they just do not give half a story.

Let's look at another poor word choice of acclaimed, experienced mediums. What do you think, gloves off or what? "Condition" is a word commonly used by many a lazy working medium (if I list them all, I'll run out of writing space) to describe any kind of illness. A fine example would be if the spirit contact passed over because of fluid on the lungs. Such a medium might weakly use the words "chest condition" to describe the illness instead of working that bit harder and getting the correct detailed diagnosis. When did it become okay to use such vague terms in our spiritual language? Agreed, it can be a huge task to correctly detail all passings, but I know from experience that spirit will give you far more descriptive evidence than "condition" and perhaps the area affected. I'm sorry, this term is just too generic. Think about it, do you go to the doctor and leave with a diagnoses of let's say an "arm condition" or "leg condition"? I don't ever recall a time when a doctor gave me medication after advising me I had something of such a vague nature. I'm sure any doctor would be struck off if they practiced that way. It is true that mediums are not doctors, so getting an exact medical term would be a miracle, but when the words "lung condition," "heart condition" or something similar are given, it's a medium's way of edging his/hers bets and stretching a given piece of evidence.

Let's be really truthful here: loved ones in spirit will give us all the fine details we need when giving evidence, but it's up to us to go after those details and deliver them to the recipient. I am exhausted by the excuses I hear daily from mediums who claim spirit only gives them certain types of evidence, or from those who spout phrases like, "I don't get that type of evidence" (meaning detailed evidence of any kind) or "Spirit doesn't give me names" (meaning full names).

Is it not strange that we live in a society where people give very little time to those who do not offer value for money, no matter the business? We have come to expect much for our money, and rightly so. My question, then, is when did working mediums get an exemption from this value for money bracket. I have said this many times before - there is no excuse any medium can give for the delivery of vague words or stretched, generic evidence. In reality, such poor work is the result of our own weaknesses, over-indulged egos, or simple lack of effort.

So back to the medium's vocabulary: the communicative and coherent delivery of accurate and detailed evidence is essential to the medium's confidence and reputation. It takes very little to be judged negatively in our field of work, and part of your job as a medium is to give the audience/client assurance that you have the ability to link with their loved ones in spirit. The only way to do this is to deliver credible evidence in clear, every day language that makes sense and leaves no room for guesswork.

No excuses - you have the ability. You just have to believe in yourself. How easy is that? A mind-thought and nothing more.

Chapter 21

Maintaining the Quality of Your Message

Be a yardstick of quality. Some people aren't used to an environment where excellence is expected.

Steve Jobs

The message portion of your one to one reading is as important as your spiritual evidence of a loved one passed over. Sometimes called guidance/psychic evidence, this portion of the communication covers details of your client's life and can either be called upon by your client or naturally flow as a part of the reading. Messages are generally dictated to the medium by the spirit contact, and can be either a large or small percentage or of the appoint-ment depending upon the client's needs. (The exception being Readers, who only wish to communicate psychically, in which case the message portion will be 100%.) No matter how the message comes about, or its content, it is important that you resist resorting to the kind of generic, off the wall rubbish that a large portion of what I like to call spiritual sharks give to their clients.

Believe me, I offer this advise from experience. I've met many workers who have given evidence to clients that left them (the clients) in such an emotional bind that they later had to seek professional counselling and/or therapy. And Debs and I are often called upon to mop up messes involving clients who have had a one to one reading with another worker and are so distraught afterward that they find it hard to carry out daily functions. Now correct me if I'm wrong, but do all spiritual workers regardless of their title not claim to come from a heavenly place and preach love and light? Well, for some I'm afraid I would have to question their sincerity.

So, how do you maintain the quality of your message? First, never take this portion of your work lightly and never skim over any evidence given from spirit. Offering a message to your client that holds some kind of forward-thinking motion for his or her life matters carries a large responsibility, as any aspect you touch on, no matter how small, can have a profound effect on your client's life. Second, remember, we are not certified psychiatrists, marriage counsellors, therapists, etc. Nor are we qualified to offer medical advice in any way. We are mediums, and so must take care not to overstep that position.

For me the message portion of my one to one reading comes in two halves - past and focus, each with its own purpose and function. Let me explain. The first half, past, covers the client's life memories (those that have already happened). Such memories can include specific details from birthdays, dates, school, relationships, names, street names, work matters, hobbies - any information that the client and only the client could know. The details of the past memories portion of a reading must carry the same quality of evidence as spirit messages from loved ones passed. There should be no slack in the quality of your evidence.

Once you have given the evidential details of the client's memories, your one to one reading should flow naturally into the guidance portion of your message - guidance being the new forward focus in your client's life matters. It is important to remember here that you are not God. The client has come to you looking for a nudge in the right direction and that's all. Keep your morals and intentions in check and never play with peoples' emotions in order to flex your mediumship ego. It is no achievement to take advantage of a client when they are emotionally weak and, as with other negative intentions, you will incur karma if your purpose is to serve your ego.

The focus, or guidance, portion should always be about the client's choices, and generally comes in in two parts, both from spirit. The first is a reflection on what the client has been and is currently going through. What part the client plays in whatever subject is being discussed or focused on in the reading is decided by spirit. How does this work? By unfolding the client's role and responsibility in those areas of his or her life, as well as any other matters he or she may have overlooked due to strong emotions or personal bias. Spirit has an uncanny way of revealing the recipient's most hidden views when it comes to dishing out guidance, and will never dismiss or cover for errors involving related events. This then leads into the second portion of the spirit message/guidanc - the client's new forward focus portion, this time from spirit. When relating guidance from spirit, always remember you are not there to directly tell the client how to live or mend his/her life. Rather, spirit enables us to offer the client choices, each with different outcomes, but all acceptable in one way or another. Each client has free will, and regardless of our input, each has a life blueprint that is his/hers alone. We cannot change that in any way, and nor should we try. Maybe what I am is as a subtle comfort. When times become difficult here on earth, mediums can remind others that our loved ones are just a thought away. Or perhaps my role is to gently nudge the client back to their life blueprint when they get a little lost in the hustle and bustle of life.

In all cases, the message or guidance portion of your one to one reading comes with a responsibility that requires a strong sense of morality, respect, and above all else pride in your work. Playing God does not make you a qualified medium. You must always respect your client's emotions and reasons for being there; they have come to you with complete trust in your work and that's what they deserve.

Chapter 22

Life's Upside Down, You Can't Think - Off to Work You Go!

The real man smiles in trouble, gathers strength from distress, and grows brave by reflection.

Thomas Paine

Many mediums offer all kinds of reasons for not being able to successfully carry out their work, whether in one to one readings or demonstrating to audiences. I think one of the most popular must be, "My life's a mess just now and I am not emotionally able to open and work with spirit." I believe it is important to discuss the emotional stressors that we have to overcome in our careers. There are, for instance, times when we have to learn to separate our personal emotions from our working sensibility in order to ensure our mediumship is always at its best. Tradition would have you believe that if, as a working medium, you are in an emotionally fragile place your mediumship will become closed off to the point that you are unable to make any links to spirit. The truth is, traditions change. Change comes from progress and progress comes from positive action. And what is positive action in mediumship? I'd say any time we reinforce a new belief or repeat an improved self-discipline or deed that results in increased productivity or directly benefits our clients - that is a positive action!

I love what I do for a living and I give my mediumship the utmost respect. In the real world, however, that is to the outside eye, it's just what I do for a living. If I'm not at my emotional best because of the stresses of everyday life, then tough as they say, I still have to go to work.

A week or so before I was about to start my first shift as a professional medium, the mother of my two daughters left me and took my two little angels with her. No more putting them to bed at night, reading them stories, or seeing to all their tears. That had to be the most heart wrenching time of my life. I love being a dad; my two daughters are my life. I had recently left the upholstery factory where I had made luxury leather furniture for the high-end market for seventeen years. Making matters worse, I had received my redundancy money, which was given to the girls' mother the moment it went into the bank. In the case of separation or divorce, British law always ensures that the mother is financially secure before the father, and so allowed her to keep the cash. Although my life was literally falling apart, there was no way I could backtrack and return to the safety of the factory, as I had already been paid off. As I was heading to work that morning, I remember thinking, "Oh my God, how am I going to do one to one readings when I can't stop crying." It was all I could do not to throw up from the upset.

Tracey and Rob, who owned the shop where I was to work, were such a fantastic couple, so supportive. For days, I would go into work red eyed after crying all-night and pining for my babies. Tracey patiently listened to my problems, and always had something positive to get me started for the day ahead. On many occasions, I kept a bath towel handy in my reading room - in between clients I held the towel to my face to dampen the noise of me crying so customers wouldn't hear it downstairs. Rob would come and check on me or let me know my next client was ready, giving me just enough time to wipe away my tears and settle down for a few seconds. Then, in the client would stroll. I've never been sure whether they had any idea what I was going through in the seconds before they entered my little reading room. What I did know was that it was my responsibility to be sure I gave the best service possible, as advertised on the shop door. I could not say, "I can't do the reading," as that was my job and my wages.

Looking back I wouldn't change the experience I had at the shop during those early days for all the tea in china. Having to stay focused and do my job taught me a valuable lesson: it does not matter what you are going through emotionally in life, you can always make that link to spirit. No excuses. They say there are only a few events in life that are that disturbing emotionally. For me being separated from my daughters is right up there. If I could work through such draining days, then so can you. Your link to your guides and spirit is always there. Each time I started a reading, the upset knot in my tummy would suppress and almost go away for the duration of the appointment, and almost the moment I finished it would come back. I'm not sure whether it was my guides or the contact for the client from spirit that calmed me. All I know is that before each reading, I said, "Take that upset away whilst I do this reading," and like clockwork it disappeared. Looking at this a little closer, I realize this was a collective effort. I authorized the want to suppress and rise above the emotion.

Once again, it goes back to what we want and believe. No matter what the circumstances in your life, you will always have the mind-set and spiritual ability to make your link to spirit, whether as part of your daily professional service or while reaching out to your loved ones passed. I agree we all have our thresholds. You will truly be surprised how high your thresholds are, given the chance to try.

Chapter 23

Practice, Practice, Practice!

Every blade of grass has an angel that bends over it and whispers 'Grow, grow.'
The Talmud

The majority of students who come to Accolade or attend any of the other thousands of workshops available globally find that it is often difficult to locate places afterwards that will help them maintain momentum in their development. I've found, however, that there are great exercises students and professional mediums alike can do on their own that will keep them motivated and energized. In fact, I would go so far as to say that some methods of in-house training are even more important than field training. That's because the only way to develop experience is through experience.

Here is an exercise I use whilst out and about or at home to support healthy rates of new mediumship evidence and maintain the quality of service insisted upon by Accolade Academy.

One to One to Myself

This is a great exercise because you can practice it wherever you are. Over the years, it's proven to be an invaluable tool and an asset to my development.

A One to One to Myself is exactly what it says on the tin, a one to one to myself. When I'm out and about travelling, I write in my notepad or type into my iPad one to one readings for individuals I randomly select from passers-by. The individual does not know about the reading and will not see what I write. Nor do I always have to see my loaned client; sometimes I just visualize someone. For instance, when we were on the plane coming home from a tour, I visualized the pilot and proceeded to do a reading for that person despite having never laid eyes on him/her. And back home in Wales there is a train track that passes in the distance. Although we cannot see the train from our home, I can hear it, and so, when time allows, I will, upon hearing the whistle, visualize the train engineer or a passenger.

In doing this exercise yourself, set a time and a goal for each reading; usually once I have selected my loaned client I will then decide how much of the reading I want to spend on spiritual evidence of a loved one passed, and how much on a message or guidance. I usually break this down into percentages that I write at the top of the page. Then set a page limit, as this will control the amount of space or time you have, just like a real reading. This creates a need for you to condense your evidence, and allows you to practice giving greater detail in the time you have with your client.

From there, the sky's the limit as they say. I often let my thoughts go and write whatever comes to mind, never holding back regardless of how my cautious mind might feel about the evidence written. This is your time to grow your confidence and courage within your evidence. I insist on thinking outside of the box during this exercise, refusing as much as I can the use of any evidence already presented that week, month or year. Use this exercise to work on your weaknesses. If you feel that one of your weaknesses is working with young clients, and having to deliver just spiritual evidence for that young person, or if names, relationships, illnesses, or the message part of evidence are difficult, put that at the top of the page with your percentage split before you start. Imagine the client has requested information from an area you find hard to access, evidence that you feel is out of your experience. Go for it! Picture this in your mind as a reading that will blow your loaned client away - the perfect one to one reading.

Another helpful aspect of this exercise is tracking the progress of your development, so keeping good records is essential. Over time, I look back through my in-house training notes and compare readings. Doing so gives a true assessment of progress made, as it is easy to see the areas in which you've grown more confident, as well as how your thoughts and feelings have expanded. As with any task, the more you practice the easier it gets. This in-house training will naturally spill over into your fieldwork, becoming part of your everyday work with evidence. Once begun, you will be surprised by the speed of this process if you practice regularly and trust the results. If you find getting out to be a problem, you can use a loaned client from a magazine - just don't choose someone famous.

The idea is to use otherwise idle time to expand your bank of mediumship knowledge and explore the thoughts that you might hold back whilst working with an actual client or audience for fear of being incorrect. This exercise allows you to stretch yourself without pressure, and in many cases this is when you will be at your best. Now, I can hear you asking, "What's the point of offering evidence if I'm not getting feedback from anybody?" Well here's the thing, a singer practices before a show, and an athlete trains before an event.

Even doctors train before becoming qualified physicians. They all participate in actions that help them gain experience before the experience. This is your form of experience before the experience. This exercise is not about feedback, but about expanding your thoughts and feelings, allowing yourself the freedom to deliver evidence or give a message that you might otherwise feel supersedes your experience.

If it works for me then why not you?

Chapter 24

The Secret to a Good Demonstration

Why should any phenomenon be assumed impossible? The Universe begins to look more and more like a great thought, than a great machine.

James Howard Jeans 1877 - 1946

There are three very important ingredients to the delivery of your evidence that will make your demonstrations as efficient and easy as possible:

1. Maintain the quality of your evidence

2. Keep your evidence interesting

3. Hold the energy

Stay within the perimeters of these three ground rules and you should always do well.

Let's look at them one at time. Number one, quality of evidence, speaks for itself, and is a subject we touch upon many times in this book. Numbers two and three must always complement one another, as they work very much as a team. Keeping evidence interesting is not just about the quality of evidence; it's about how well that evidence is presented to the audience. If you have a venue that holds let's say a hundred or so people, there will always be a percentage of the audience that will loose interest at some point whilst you are working with an individual. Demonstrating mediumship can get very boring visually for the seated audience. I have seen many people fall asleep whilst watching mediums work.

To make sure that doesn't happen to you, remember that your job is not just to deliver evidence to one individual, but also to deliver it in a way that engages the rest of the audience at the same time. Let me explain what I mean by this. Say you are on stage and you have both your contact from spirit and a recipient in the audience. You feel you have a great link, and deliver evidence that gets plenty of positive feedback from your recipient. Now here's the thing - unless your evidence is completely clear and understandable on all levels to the rest of the audience then they will no longer be able to actively participate. You need to be aware of the words and terminology used within your delivery. You see, once you have your recipient and he/she acknowledges and accepts that the contact you have from spirit does belong to them, then truthfully, if you are doing your job correctly, your focus should shift the delivery of your message to the whole audience. You are delivering a message to one person, yes, but in such a way that everybody in the audience has a complete understanding of what it is you are describing, explaining, and delivering.

How would this work? Let's say you purchase an item that requires assembly instructions. The assembly instructions must be clear and universal so that people from all walks of life can follow them. On that particular day of assembling your item, the instructions belong to you and act as your personal guide, but they must be user-friendly for everyone. Just like the assembly instructions need to be understood by all who read them, your delivery is intended for all in the audience. But at the same time it must remain very personal to the individual you are linking with. Your choice of words must be universal and explicit. Remember, just because the one recipient you are working with is giving you great positive feedback this does not mean the exchange is interesting to watch or hear for the rest of the audience. Your job is to keep it interesting, and this will in turn keep the audience excited and energized.

One of the best pieces of advice I give to our students is for them to keep their links short whilst demonstrating. I have seen many mediums work with the same individual in an audience for up to ten, maybe even fifteen minutes. I mean, come on ladies and gents, this has to be like watching paint dry for other audience members hoping to get their own contact from spirit. When a medium spends that amount of time with the one person it's often because they are getting plenty of reassuring yes responses from their recipient. The more time they spend with one individual the more they are in danger of totally exhausting and over-stretching the message. This is when the worker needs to recognize his/her ego has taken over his/her mediumship. Sometimes, this can also be due to a lack in confidence; they stay with this exhausted positive link on the hope of passing time just in case the next link is not as good.

Another thing I tell students is to time themselves. As a medium, you should aim for an average of three minutes per link. You can have plenty of conversation in three minutes. Try it. If you go over that's okay, as keeping an average is good enough. When Debs and I demonstrate together we have a customary tap that we give to each other as discretely as possible as a signal to say the link has gone on long enough. There may be times the link insists on more time due to the sensitivity of the evidence being given, and that's fine as well. Just be aware always of time spent with each individual. Maintaining discipline in this regard will help so much in keeping the energy alive in the audience.

Which brings us to number three: hold the energy. Many a practicing medium adopts an inflated sense of expectation when aiming to hold the energy during demonstrations. I mean, just the words "holding the energy" totally confused me for many years. Did this mean holding my breath, or keeping up some kind of angelic uplift I could not for the life of me feel? The words were too vague and did not really explain or instruct me in any way as to what I needed to do in order to hold the energy whilst demonstrating. Truthfully, I have not met one working medium who could explain in simple words how the mechanics of this process works. At least not in a way made that made any real sense without sounding like I needed angel wings for the goal to be achievable.

So once again I was left to work this one out for myself. Here is the explanation I came up with in its simplest format: to hold the energy for me means keeping control of the evening, being in charge of the audience, and making sure I am always confident in the delivery and the clarity of my message. Always remember, regardless of your profile or your popularity, if people have paid to see you work they will feel you owe them something, which, truthfully, you do. You owe them a professional service during the time they spend with you. After all they have paid and that payment is your wages.

So how do we keep control of a demonstration, getting the long awaited standing ovation once finished, and leaving the audience wanting more once the evening is over? Well, these come when you offer something the audience has never experienced before - a way of working that is above the norm, as they say. As if our jobs are not stressful enough. Hey, that's the life of a publicly owned product, more commonly known as the professional psychic medium.

As mediums, we must always think on our feet, learn to analyze our audience, and know that our last demonstration will be dated on our return visit. Your job is to continue to introduce new evidence with a fresh delivery to complement that evidence.

I for one love double links and sharing my links with Debs. Whether you demonstrate with another medium or as an individual, double links are great fun. This is an easy process, no different really than holding a two-way conversation, something we all do in life. Think of it as speaking to two or more people on various subjects whilst out socializing with a group of friends. A double link is no different, except the words given from you come from more than one contact from spirit. You will feel a difference in the links and, with a little practice you will learn to know which contact belongs to which recipient. This way of working keeps the audience on edge, wondering who is next and when. Just remember, keep it under control. Don't open too many links as that can get you into a mess.

Debs and I generally like to open with maybe two or three links to start a demonstration, as this brings excitement to the evening almost instantly. This energy is passed from you to the audience and from them right back to you. Occasionally, after starting one link, I may hold the close of that link until ever so slightly later in the demonstration, as this helps keep the energy high. This energy then creates a sense of urgency that both the individual recipient and the audience will send out as a result of their desire for us to return to and finish the message. We call this manipulating the energy. We've been told the late Gordon Higginson, who is considered one of the UK's best mediums of all time, practiced this method. Higginson was one of the Arthur Findley College's (Stanstead Hall) greatest teaching mediums and leaders. Higginson would go to one section of the audience, open a link by validating both his contact and the recipient who the contact belonged to in the audience, and then start the message with something profound and detailed from spirit. Then he'd ask if the link could "hold that thought" for a few minutes whilst he finished or opened another link elsewhere in the audience (generally at the opposite end of the hall as this builds even more excitement).

The aim of this exercise is always to benefit the audience, not your ego. Please don't use this advice as an excuse to overdo any party tricks, as your intent is what's important here. It is your job to create an atmosphere that is valuable to the audience, which in turn will make your job much easier. Think of it this way: have you ever been to a wedding reception that was very slow, with little fun or excitement? Somehow, the guests just never got to a place that helped create an energized atmosphere, thus enabling those special wedding photos we all cringe at after having too many alcoholic beverages. Then there's the wedding reception that is so fantastic that nobody wants to go home because everybody is having a blast. Well, your job is to create the feel of the latter without the alcohol, leaving the audience with the memory of wanting more, regardless of how difficult they may have been.

Many a medium has asked us if we feel we are "disrespecting spirit" when working with more than one member of the audience at a time. How could that be? Are we not designed as a people to enjoy events and times that reawaken that loving nostalgic feel of recognition in our lives? It feeds a sense of wellbeing in both the audience and the loved ones in spirit, as I am sure they did not loose the need to feel this awareness when passing over. As a demonstrating medium my job is to deliver exact evidence in a way that involves as many audience members as possible. I trust my guides and those I represent from spirit, and I assume they trust me, or my style just would not come to fruition. Besides, why does a demonstration have to be a stuffy event? Yes, you are totally correct - our job is not to create a cabaret evening. Balance is vital to provide the respect needed for those receiving messages from loved ones passed. Some recipients can be very sensitive and a gentle approach supersedes all else. Giving evidence from the many different personalities you will encounter from spirit requires a little practice, as each deserves to be represented in all his/her essence. Learn to be comfortable when working with personalities and evidential memories from those in spirit - particularly those who switch from one extreme to the other. Trust the process; balance will be given in a way that will fit the needs of the audience not you.

So long as you keep your ego out of the way and maintain respect for your audience, you will do just fine. You'll see.

Chapter 25

My Demonstrations

Use this space to make a truthful self-analysis of how individ-ual demonstrations go for you, dividing each event into five sections.

Date of Event:

Run Up to the Event:

Start of the Event:

Midpoint:

Final Stages:

Post Event:

Date of Event:

Run Up to the Event:

Start of the Event:

Midpoint:

Final Stages:

Post Event:

Date of Event:

Run Up to the Event:

Start of the Event:

Midpoint:

Final Stages:

Post Event:

Date of Event:

Run Up to the Event:

Start of the Event:

Midpoint:

Final Stages:

Post Event:

Date of Event:

Run Up to the Event:

Start of the Event:

Midpoint:

Final Stages:

Post Event:

Chapter 26

The Answer is Never NO: Just Look Again

I have learned that success is to be measured not so much by the position that one has reached in life as by the obstacles which he has had to overcome while trying to succeed.
                                               Booker T. Washington

The word "No" has enormous power in our language and can undermine much of our confidence. It is the dreaded word we all hate to hear from a client when giving any kind of evidential mediumship, and it has finished many a good medium's career.

Perhaps the strongest two-letter word that any developing psychic medium will ever have to overcome, "No" can be delivered to the psychic medium from all kinds of personalities in a way that can and does dictate variations of control between the client/audience and the psychic medium.

What's even harder about No is that it is a not just a word, but a memory. It's an inheritance from our and our parents' upbringing. It's also the word we use to recall instilled familiarities and emotions that cause personal experiences to resurface. It's an opinionated word that allows the biases of others to creep into our presentation. When we hear the word no, many of our childhood doubts explode back to life in an instant. But it can also be very subtle, enough so that it allows negative intentions to take over and weaken your confidence.

The word no is very clever. It pretends it's a protective, loyal guardian that will reward you with feel-good authoritarian stripes, but remember each time you use this negative word in everyday speech there has to be a consequence. As with all negatives, karma insists the safe return to its rightful owner.

Starting out as a working medium I had to analyze the word no in my life and career until I was able remove the power of negativity and replace it with a word that allows me to hold onto my confidence. I knew I couldn't dictate my client's language or request that he or she answer using only words I find comfortable. Instead, I trained myself to hear another word whenever a no is delivered. The secret, I've learned, lies in remembering that when I receive a no, it actually means LOOK AGAIN. Yes, look again. How easy that is? You see, your client is not asking you to stop (unless they literally do request you to "stop"). They are asking you to go back and try again. We often hear 'no' voiced in our direction, but in such situations, we have a choice as to how to receive that no, as well as how to respond.

In this case, it is important to learn how to program your confidence to enjoy the word 'no' each time it is sent in your direction. Regardless of the level of intensity when working, see 'no' as part of your positive training, an opportunity without which you would have little opportunity for advancement in the growth of your evidence. This is true whether you're in a one to one reading or demonstrating to a live audience. Rely on the same repeated format, never stretching your mediumship or the clarity of your evidence. Think of 'no' as your most loyal teacher. When I get a 'no', I tell myself it's my favourite, most trusting guide, helping me improve my services to my customer. So bring it on, as they say. Keep taking the 'no's, and remember they only have the strength you allow them.

Chapter 27
Ego Within Your Work

Only from the heart can you touch the sky.
                              Jalal Uddin Rumi 1207 – 1272

We are choked by the use of the word ego within our beloved spiritual movement. I often ask myself why this is. Have we forgotten that a healthy ego plays a huge part in our working careers? I for one love my ego. Without it, I would have very little hope of sustaining confidence in any aspect of my evidential presentations, the conducting of one to one readings, teaching, or any of the finer details of my work in general. I agree that there is way too much ego within most spiritual movements, but I believe that this overabundance is usually generated from a lack of confidence, stemming from a negative ego rather than a positive ego. What do I mean by a negative and positive ego? First let's look at the negative.

The negative ego is usually seen in individuals who hold very little trust in their work and will make any excuse to justify their inability to produce quality mediumship. A fine example is the medium who blames the recipient for his or her own lack of quality evidence, claiming the recipient is wrong to refuse such evidence when the recipient clearly does not recognize the information given by the medium. At the same time, the medium insists that spirit would never give him/her any evidence that was wrong. The favourite follow-up line seems to be, "Take that piece of evidence home with you, I'm sure it will fit somewhere." You see, a negative ego is grown over time and often presents itself in a positive disguise, cleverly giving the impression of confidence in its human carrier. I almost make the negative ego sound like a disease, and truthfully it can become like that! The need to elevate oneself through false impressions can become a constant, synthetic reality, clouding the medium's true level of development or working experience. At the same time, a negative ego attempts to sell unearned respect to the naïve in order to broadcast one's make-believe confidence to the spiritual community, thus earning the ego carrier some degree of juvenile ranking.

I can't stress this enough: please, please, please don't get involved with such negative practices. It is easy to slip into an attitude of false pride, which can in turn be very damaging to both your clients and your reputation. Regardless of how light the exaggeration, karma will catch up with you at some point and bring that negative ego crashing down. How do I know? Well, I have been there myself. It took some practice for me to get my negative ego in check. I wish someone had given me this advice in the very beginning of my practice, so that I could have avoided embarrassing myself.

So let's lift the tone a little and look at the secret to a positive, or healthy, spiritual ego. What is a healthy spiritual ego? In my opinion it is self-love, but a genuine self-love that wants to nurture confidence in order to benefit others. A healthy ego wants to become even more confident and progressive with its skills and experiences. In return, this creates an evolutionarily perfect educational experience for those developing within their mediumship.

How can we grow our healthy ego? Firstly, we must see our faults, looking to ourselves when we have a bad day at the spiritual office. Often, we spend too much time blaming clients and their attitudes, or we use some excuse (maybe not having the correct breakfast, or not eating enough or too much). Believe me, I have heard so many crazy excuses for mediums not being able to make a great link on a given day. I've often wondered how such excuses would hold up with a regular employer. Could we say, "I couldn't make the daily targets as I had too many bowls of cereal for breakfast"? I mean think about it - does it really matter how much or how little we eat? Truth is, there is not an excuse we can legitimately offer for poor results beyond our own shortcomings.

That's not to say the client has nothing to do with the results we produce, because you are still only as good as your recipient. I have sat with many clients and been absolutely sure I was correct, but still been told "NO" in a "You will never be correct" manner. What can you do in that situation, other than swallow your pride and end the appointment? As my Debs often says, "Paul, some clients just don't want to be read." Their aim is to justify their desire to trash any form of psychic ability, including mediumship. We are all entitled to our opinions, of course, and a healthy ego will allow you to handle such situations. If you are in charge, gracefully extracting yourself will be of no detriment to your ability. If a client has no wish to be read then don't read them. Perhaps the next time round their attitude will be somewhat different and more accommodating. That does not mean you should not work for your money, but you are not a psychic punching bag either.

You see, growing a healthy ego comes from having the ability to hold such trust in your mediumship and career path that you will not have the need to impose such phrases as "I am the best" or "I also gave the same great evidence to that recipient." One of the most common ego boosters by far is the exaggerated, full appointments diary boast: "My appointments diary is full for the next few months, and I now have a waiting list" or "I'm not sure how I will meet my workload." The purpose of these boasts, of course, is to sound as if one is so well liked that he/she cannot possibly keep up with the demands of his/her popularity. This in turn expels the energy of the conversation in the direction of the poor, inexperienced victim, as the medium seeks to elevate his/herself to the level of a Hollywood superstar. Believe me, I've seen and heard this many times. Listen to yourself as you talk about your mediumship. Are you exaggerating, or being truthful? What is your intent in having the discussion? Is it simply to gain that feel-good factor on the back of someone else's lack of knowledge? Or do you have a sincere desire to help in some way?

Have you ever gone to a house party and heard a plumber bragging about the amount of copper pipe he used whilst carrying out his duties? Or a dentist happily holding the room, sharing with all the speed at which she removed a client's tooth? What's the benefit to the speaker in such conversations? More than likely, it will sound as though the dentist's only interest is to get her clients in and out as fast as possible, without prioritizing their care in the least. The same goes for the plumber - being, or even seeming to be, super speedy or expensive is not the best form of service. In fact, such inflated talk often damages the speaker. It is, of course, important to enjoy your achievements in life and work, and to share them with those who carry an interest. But please remember, there is a fine balance between reality and fiction, and it's your responsibility to find and maintain that balance. A negative ego never holds any reward in your chosen mediumship career. And once obtained, it can be one of the most damaging traits you will ever have to overcome.

So there you have it, easy peasy. To maintain a healthy ego that will complement your mediumship and improve your quality of life, resist using weak, self-inflated statements.

Always be truthful, be proud of your current level of mediumship, and never use your experience to intimidate others.

Chapter 28
Why Do We Need to Brag?

The Lord can do great things through those who don't care who gets the credit.

Helen Pearson

I'm never really sure what to offer society in terms of a job description for my career. Am I a medium? A psychic? Or maybe a sensitive? I could keep it simple and say I'm an individual who uses his intuition a little more than others. When applying for insurance or filling out any kind of legal document, there is never a title that covers us mediums. I suppose this kind of puts us in no man's land, as we are employed by an unknown service. No wonder the everyday world has an uneasy time accepting our existence. We are for many the secret appointment no one talks about - that underground whisper.

In a way, we are our own worst enemies. Mediums past and present are to blame and no one else; long ago, the movement became obsessed with the desire to proclaim that the ability to link with loved ones passed is a process for none but the individually gifted, a belief that continues today. As a result, respected intuitive workers worldwide became the invisible heroes of their times. Not for a second am I disrespecting our many fantastic mediums, but I believe our role is to reawaken the memory of this ability in as many people as we can reach, reinforcing the fact that natural intuitive mediumship can only result in a positive outlook on life. How wonderful it is to know that those we miss so much are always there with us - it really is a no brainer as they say.

The problem started when some in the movement of spiritualism who supported mediumship (or the independent medium) became self-absorbed. In selfishly promoting their individual, out-of-the-ordinary image and claiming ownership over the ability to use mediumship, they added to the mystic reputation already in place. Hoping to keep mediumship as theirs alone, they further removed it from the everyday radar of common acceptance. These workers like to call themselves professional advocators for mediumship, ignoring the fact that mediumship is not about the medium, but the bigger picture of the clarity of everlasting existence.

Let's put this another way: is my role as a father about me? No my job as a Dad is to unselfishly prepare my daughters for their future the best I can, to bring them an understanding that life is much bigger than their Dad, and that I am just a stepping stone of reassurance for them. A Dad is no more than the advertising board of life, as a medium is no more than the advertising board of spirituality.

So what name can we use to foster acceptance of this age-old practice whilst also proudly promoting professionalism within our industry, allowing it to sit side by side with the most successful of globally recognized businesses. Perhaps this then would remove the mystic chill of distrust a sceptical public is accustomed to feeling when the titles medium or psychic are offered. I'm not sure I have the answers. Maybe we can start with the senior mediums within spiritualism, or the high profile, independent mediums who claim ownership of their ability to link to spirit (as if it was some kind of one in a million gift). To them, I would like to say, "Stop! Make it your goal in life to share what you have but in a real way. A way that can be understood by people from all walks of life, not just your groupies." Mediums everywhere must bring their work back down to earth. After all, how the hell can we expect to earn professional recognition if our "leaders" (those we choose to follow) cannot control their egos?

I agree that heroes and leaders are necessary in any movement or business, but surely we need ground troops first. Our industry does not have a strong enough, or large enough, customer base to compete with the local football team, so why the need for so many coaches? Or why the seemingly unlimited desire to lead a movement that has yet to become large enough to satisfy such an appetite for power? We have yet to reach the general public, yet alone the masses of our world. Any leader worth his/her salt should always want what is best for the individuals who make up their following, as well as those who look to them for guidance This I fear is what's missing in this movement. He who leads to brag leads for his gains only, he who leads to share leads for the desire to encourage another and ensure the greater good of all.

To those developing in their mediumship, I say, regardless of your working profile or your level of experience within your mediumship, it will all be meaningless if you have no movement to progress within. To the advanced worker, I say, tear off your leader stripes and get back to grassroots mediumship. We must make our mark in society, creating a reputation that allows for the acceptance of our industry, and enabling all mediums to stand proud next to the giants of the business world.

Chapter 29
Positive Affirmations Are Your Best Friend

"Your ability to imagine will help the next logical steps come to you faster. Use your imagination until your big dream feels so familiar that the manifestation is the next logical step.
Abraham-Hicks

As the technician of your mediumship, you need to keep your mind strong, finding and practicing as many mind-strengthening exercises as possible. Keeping your positive outlook and self-belief in shape with daily workouts is fantastically rewarding, because, as you know, both are major players in sustaining self-confidence and trust in your development. This is true regardless of what stage you feel you are at. If you are working professionally with your mediumship, then practicing daily affirmations should be a required activity.

Affirmations are the best complement to your new tool of positive intent, but what exactly is an affirmation? It is said that affirmations are any statements that we make - positive or negative. When used consistently, these statements become beliefs, which then shape our outlook and progress, often producing results in ways that we could not have imagined. According to this theory, thoughts come before beliefs. With each thought or affirmation being so precious, it's wise that we look at this a little closer. Here I will discuss both positive and negative affirmations, as what's important is to remove those that hold you back and replace them with new, positive affirmations that will aid your personal development. Let's start with some of the most commonly used negative affirmations. I have heard many of these from students all over the world, offered in a variety of situations.

Negative Affirmations

- I AM NOT GOOD ENOUGH.
- EVERYBODY JUDGES ME.
- MEDIUMSHIP IS EASIER FOR OTHERS.
- I WILL LOOK A FOOL.
- I DON'T HAVE "THE GIFT."
- MY EVIDENCE WILL DO.
- I CAN'T DO IT.
- OTHER PEOPLE ARE BETTER THAN ME.
- I DON'T DESERVE MEDIUMSHIP.
- I DON'T GET GOOD EVIDENCE.
- MEDIUMSHIP IS A GIFT I DON'T HAVE.
- I AM UNWORTHY.
- I HAVE NEVER BEEN GOOD AT ANYTHING.
- I WILL LET SPIRIT DECIDE MY PATH.
- I DON'T HAVE THE COURAGE TO DO MEDIUMSHIP.
- MEDIUMSHIP IS ONLY FOR THE FEW.
- I DON'T GET NAMES WHEN I AM LOOKING FOR EVIDENCE.

Many negative affirmations are the unspoken doubts that students think and feel but don't actually say to others.

Whether spoken or thought, they are confidence-crushers that we freely authorize to sabotage our confidence.

How many of the above do you recognize in yourself? I know there were a few for me when I first started. If you don't find your negative affirmations in the list above, take a moment to think about your confidence-crushers. Be as truthful as you can with yourself, writing each as they come to you. Once exposed, they can be removed.

Positive Affirmations

When using or working with positive affirmations it is good practice to have one or two foundation-setters, using the others randomly throughout your day or week. I have found an affirmation works best when strength is given to the subtlest of thoughts. For me, the danger in speaking an affirmation aloud is that I then run the risk of stressing about its intensity and wondering if I've done enough to make it sink in. I find myself going through the process over and over until the whole exercise becomes a negative in itself. Also, I've found speech to be the weakest of ways to strengthen either my thoughts or mediumship.

You see, many parts of our mediumship/intuition work by thoughts, and on many levels within our thoughts. So it is there, in your thoughts, that you must practice your affirmation workout. As you present each positive affirmation in the lightest of thoughts, that affirmation will grow into a larger thought, eventually becoming an every day, naturally occurring belief. Let this happen intuitively. Don't overthink your exercise. Over time, the affirmation will become a knowing rather than a statement of need.

What do I mean by a knowing? A knowing is the same feeling or understanding I have that gives me the unquestioned belief that I am Paul Rees and that night comes after day or day comes after night. It's that simple.

In my opinion many people who talk about the power of positive thinking go about it the wrong way, claiming that positive energy is created by the largest thoughts or by expressing those thoughts from voice to universe. How can that be when our largest thoughts are very singular and short-lived? Our smaller thoughts contain more detail, carrying us through our subconscious day and creating a sense of self-love, life trust, individual confidence, personal knowledge and all the other energies that we as individuals sometimes fail to notice, but that stand out to others.

So start your new workout today! Here is a list of positive affirmations that I use, courtesy of my dear wife. (Thank you Debs xx.) I find this list more than adequate, as using or relying on too many affirmations weakens the process and purpose of the exercise. Your list can be added to as needed.

- I AM A FANTASTIC PERSON.
- I AM GOOD ENOUGH TO BE A MEDIUM.
- I DESERVE MY MEDIUMSHIP.
- I AM A LOVING PERSON.
- I AM A FANTASTIC MEDIUM.
- I ONLY HAVE GOOD THOUGHTS ABOUT MYSELF.
- I GIVE PEACE TO PEOPLE.
- I GET WONDERFUL EVIDENCE.
- I AM LOVABLE.
- MEDIUMSHIP COMES EASY TO ME.
- I WAS BORN WITH THIS ABILITY.
- I FEEL WORTHY.
- I AM A MIRACLE.
- I ONLY HAVE GOOD THOUGHTS ABOUT OTHERS.

- I HAVE THE COURAGE TO DO MEDIUMSHIP.
- GOD SMILED THE DAY I WAS BORN.

There you have it. Get working with your new affirmations. Transform your thoughts so that you can become all that you already are and much more.

Chapter 30
My Positive Affirmations

Use this space to record your positive affirmations. Your affirmations will change over time, depending upon which areas you feel need a boost in confidence. Make new lists as necessary.

My Positive Affirmations:

Chapter 31
What Is A Guide?

The wisdom of the ages teaches that each individual, whether believer or not, good or bad, old or young, sick or well, rich or poor, has a personal Guardian Angel with him or her at every moment of life.

I had never heard of guides before I started on my current spiritual path and began educating myself via the vast array of literature available on the subject. I had, of course, heard of Guardian Angels, who I always imagined as being big-winged, golden-lit, ten-foot tall Goddess-like creatures sent down to Earth to look after me in times of trouble. Seriously, that was the extent of my understanding of guides right up to the age of thirty-one.

That was when I came to understand that guides are spirit beings that volunteer to be our unseen best friends and constant companions. Some guides come and go, while others are there throughout our lives. This is the case with our main guides, who are with us from before we incarnate. One of their purposes is to discuss with us in great detail the specifics of our coming life, including what we hope to gain from our time on Earth and what virtues we would like to keep when we depart. From our first breath on this Earth in this lifetime until, and even beyond, our last breath, our main guide will have the most spiritual input in our lives. Their main purpose is to try and keep us on the path we have mapped out for this particular lifetime, often by helping us reach the goals our spirit has set for itself. Whenever we veer off track, it is part of their commitment to us to help steer us back on the right path, via both synchronicity and, I believe, by influencing our thoughts. Have you ever had a really bright idea that seemed to appear out of nowhere just when you really needed it? Such thoughts mostly come through the help of your guide. That is not to say your guides are in control of your decisions. No matter how much we map out our lives, I believe we can get an A on our life-plan or a D. This is because we still have freewill, and the choices we make each day are ours alone.

As we become more spiritually aware and start to work in service, other guides assign themselves to us, or were pre–assigned by us before we incarnated, for the purpose of helping with a particular role within our life's work. This form of guide could be there, for instance, to help me in my mediumship when I am communicating with the other side. If I decide to go down the path of spiritual healing or of spiritual art then another guide would direct this portion of my work, leaving day to day life matters to my main guide. As I say, these guides are not static; as we evolve spiritually during our life on Earth, we receive different guides to help us along the way.

We determine whatever life lessons we would like to learn or, as I like to say acquire, in childhood. We choose our parents and early life situations according to who and what generally will present the complete opposite situations to the aspects we are trying to acquire. For example, if we want to gain self-love, then we will have a childhood without anyone to mirror our inner or outer beauty back to us and have that as our companion for the first few years. Or perhaps our early years are wonderful and we feel loved and cherished. Then we get out into the world and find it is totally different and we are not treated so nicely. It's easy in such circumstances to begin to distrust all that we've been taught about ourselves. Now comes the hard process of believing in yourself, trusting your own judgment, and staying true to what you know about yourself despite your new surroundings and a lack of understanding from others.

Most spirits choose to experience the opposite situations to the attribute/attributes we are endeavouring to acquire how to in their childhood. This is because the attribute/attributes are not just then reacquired during life, but have been earned from scratch and therefore have more worth. Also the human brain and the emotional body (intellect and emotion are mainly opposites, yet remain closely connected) are like computers; whatever is programmed in first will be the automatic response forever (in this lifetime) unless we change the programming. And changing the programming is what our spirit is up to; it is the point of life. I also believe that the more evolved the spirit, the harder the aspect/aspects it will seek to obtain. Therefore, they generally choose harder life situations to overcome. The ultimate outcome of any incarnation would be to fully realize the spirit within ourselves, to have it overpower the personality part of us. This would allow us go beyond the subconscious and conscience mind and operate entirely through what scientists call the super-conscience, or as I like to put it, our Godliness, and then create a life in the body from that state of awareness and have the Heaven on Earth we are all searching for.

In life, situations arise again and again (offering an opportunity to overcome circumstances and thus gain the attribute/attributes), as we do not always have the courage, knowledge, or desire to go back and change the program. Instead, such circumstances hold us back, causing pain and heartache to us as well as others. Look to your life - what circumstances repeatedly show up? The answer(s) to this question will offer definite clues as to what aspects you are trying to gain in this lifetime.

Throughout this process, our guides stay with us, trying to nudge us in the right direction and even offering thoughts that we then think are our own. Guides will never stand in front of us and tell us what to do. That is not their job; they are called guides, because that is all they are there to do.

It is also important to remember that our guides love us more than we love ourselves. They know exactly who we are. They know we are not our personalities and they know we are not our human selves, full of weakness and judgment. They are familiar with our selfishness and stubborn self-righteousness and understand that it is precisely these things that we have come to this harsh planet to overcome. I call this planet harsh on the grounds that we arrive here from home - a place where inner peace and overwhelming love for others and ourselves is the norm - only to be thrown into an alien environment where we feel alone and separate. This is a devastating shock to the spirit, yet a necessary one if we are to become evolved and merge back with the one.

Only guides know our true agenda here, along with our life plan - what I like to call the blueprint of our life. Their job is to help us not only stick to that path but to surpass the expected outcome. In this way, I believe they are here to help us act for our highest good in a crisis, to help us take appropriate action and not make mistakes that will incur huge amounts of karma. (I believe karma, good or bad, is earned along the way in this life too.) Mainly, I believe they are here to remind us who we really are, based upon our worth not only as spirits but as human beings as well.

This does not mean that guides are here to "fix" our every problem. Nor are they assigned to us in order to sort out any emotional or physical difficulties, however large or small. They may nudge us in the right direction only. They cannot shield us from the life we have chosen; if pain, either physical or emotional, comes our way then it must come, for that is what we asked for before we were born. It is my belief that nothing in life is random and nothing happens by accident. I have often wondered what it must be like to be a guide to someone, and I tell you it takes a brave spirit for that path. And not only brave - our guides must also be more evolved than us. I like to think this is true by a very large margin, but I have met others who don't share that view. Rather they seem to think that as long as our guides are even a little more evolved than us, then that is enough.

Perhaps I just need the safety of a good few thousand years of evolvement between my guide and me! J Imagine you're a guide to someone that you love as you would love your own child and that they are about to go through something terrible, either physically or emotionally. Now imagine that you have to stand by and let that experience happen. Although you know your loved one is not in serious danger, being that they are a spirit and will live forever, right now they are under the illusion that this earthly life is their "real" life. As such they have a horrible sense of sadness, fear or doom. How brave must one be to not interfere, to not stop the process, to not make your charge escape somehow or change course in order to avoid that terrible something. I guess sometimes guides have to remind themselves that such things happen for the greater good. But to my mind, it takes a special soul to be a guide, given the inhumane atrocities that some of us endure while on this planet.

Please do show your guides some respect! They have been with you through all that you have endured, often suffering right along with you. And now that you know they are present, don't fall into the trap many people do: guides are not genies. Don't call on them to make this or that person fall in love with you, or to save a pair of shoes that you like in the store until you have the money to buy them. Don't ask that they get you out of a hole you have gotten into or to lessen your karma for any reason. And absolutely no shouting at them when things don't go right in your life - especially if you've had one too many.

The role of our guides is to keep us on the path of our blueprint as much as possible. To remind us that all problems exist for a reason, and all offer an opportunity for spiritual growth. Guides will help bring you to your own conclusions about life, and to evolve as much as possible in one lifetime here on our beautiful Earth.

And just HOW they do this? Through our thoughts, plain and simple. They are, to me, truly the unsung heroes, particularly the millions of guides who never get acknowledged, not even a slight acknowledgement that they are there during one's lifetime. That, people, is what I call service.

Chapter 32

How I Got To Know My Guides

You should never feel lonely, neglected, fearful, or defeated when you remember that there are the shining ones. They are watching with keen interest and a great desire to help to raise you, to stimulate you into contact with your own superior inner resources.

Flower A. Newhouse 1909 – 1994

I first heard about the possibility that all of us living on Earth had at least one being who would follow us through life during a weeklong residential course called The Hoffman Process, which I like to call an emotional detox. I was of course very curious to know who my guides were, as I believe everyone, when starting such a journey, has an overwhelming need to know who is guiding them.

There are some who teach in spiritualist centres that the identity of our guides is of no importance. Just go with the flow, they say, as long as you feel comfortable in your work there is no need to know anything about your guides. I agree with the fact there is no real reason. We do not need to know who our guides are in order to work as a medium. They love us regardless and have the utmost respect for our work. Your guide will make absolutely no judgments of you, your thoughts or your behaviour in this life. After all, it is your spirit who has the handicap of being in a physical body, with a physical brain, human emotions and your previously mapped life-agenda to work through.

The point some teachers miss is the reason why some of us want to know our guides. It is not mere curiosity that drives us. Rather, we realize that this might be our only chance to have a relationship with someone who loves us unconditionally in this life. The thought that a guide is assigned to us exclusively makes us feel special. It is great to know we are the most important person in the world to someone, without question and without risk of losing them, no matter what. Feeling special and loved in this way is what we look for here on Earth. Because let's face it, if humans were able to love each other unconditionally and without prejudices there would be no point to us incarnating at all.

There is also the very real fact that we are bonded with our guides as souls, and that underneath our personality in this life we know and love them in the exact same way as they know and love us. For this reason, your guide is like an old friend on the very edge of your earthly mind, one that we unconsciously feel and know is there.

Not long after I first heard about guides, I attended a spiritual art class. I was very excited, as the tutor explained that she would show us a technique to gain the help and influence of our guide. Telling us to close our eyes, she instructed that we ask our guides to help us draw them. Just as spirit can influence our thoughts when we are giving evidence during one to one readings or demonstrations. As I drew, I felt like I was on autopilot; I did not know what part I would visualize next. To my amazement I drew really fast, too fast for my mind to contemplate what I was doing. This was a good thing, as I knew that my guide was helping me with the process. I was so surprised with the outcome! The finished sketch was very good. Though it was no Monet, it was still a thousand times better than I could have ever drawn by myself. I am very much the stick man type of artist!

Looking at the finished product, it was clear that my guide was an Oriental of some sort, not Chinese or Japanese yet similar. I could not tell if it was a male or female, as it appeared very feminine yet with definite masculine overtones. Hmmm... I had to find out more. I had been told that if you want to ask your guide for a name it is important to quiet your mind as much as possible. By this, I mean sitting and remaining conscious, yet trying not to think about anything specific. This may initially be difficult, as the main function of the brain and what it is programmed to do is think. Yet, with practice, we can get to a stage where the mind is empty of all thought, although learning to hold that state of quietness of mind for any length of time can take years. If you use this method, do not TRY to stop your thoughts, as such an effort keeps you in control of thoughts and so more aware of them. The trick is to imagine yourself as an observer, let your thoughts float in and float out. Concentrating on your breathing also helps. Pay attention as you breathe in, and as you breathe out. Breath actually has no content, so although you can concentrate on its flow, there is nothing to actually think about.

As you become more aware of yourself as an observer, your attention to the thoughts themselves will lessen. And as you find thoughts becoming less frequent, you will become more in touch with your spirit, and thus more receptive to the pure thoughts of other spirits. These pure thoughts will come in clearly, without being filtered through your own. This is why "sitting in the power" is considered to be very different from meditation. For sitting in the power will enable you to quickly come to, or near to, the state of mind necessary for working and giving messages.

So, as instructed, I sat with the intention of being told my guide's name. In a silence absent of my own thoughts I heard the words "Chung Yoi." I had no idea if this was a name, but I went with it. As I began calling my guide Chung Yoi, I felt he/she/it become more familiar. One day, friends of mine told me they were going to China for a trip. This was my chance, I thought! I asked if they would take the words with them and inquire whilst there if this was indeed a name. My fear was that Chung Yoi could be gobbledygook, or that the phrase might mean loaf of bread, couch or even wheelie bin. As I say, I had no idea at all during this time in evolution.

My friends were away in China for a few weeks so I had to be patient, something that is not a strong point of mine. I was delighted when they came back from the trip and reported that the name meant "Youth Fervour, Love and Stamina"! How brilliant was that? At the time I did not yet know the true meaning of this name for myself, but I liked it.

Now nine years later Youth Fervour makes perfect sense. It is the mission of Accolade Academy to train as many young people to be qualified as mediums as possible. Our mission takes lots of love and stamina, requiring a youthful, almost childlike and constant enthusiasm. For the last four years, Paul and I have being working 15 to 16 hour days to build Accolade into a successful, far-reaching venture. And this folks is just the beginning!

So there I was, finally comfortable in the knowledge that my guide was named Chung Yoi. Yet I still wanted more. I had, by then, established that Chung Yoi was a male. I had studied my drawing, sat in the power and asked that my guide draw near to me. In doing so, I felt an energy that was definitely masculine. Looking back, having a male guide was the best option for me at the start of my journey, as that helped me feel safe and protected. In the early days of my awareness, security was my top priority due to my Irish Catholic upbringing and my father's strong opinions relating to contact with spirit. Today I have no such fears, nor does my mind need protection against spirit in any way. I feel slightly foolish about my earlier concerns, yet I cannot blame myself for my initial failings in trust as they were due to the warnings against any contact with spirit that were taught to me during my childhood.

My next desire was to discover where Chung Yoi had lived while he was on the Earth. I took a map of the world, and hovered a pendulum over Asia and the Far East. (A pendulum is a weight hung from a fixed point so that it can swing freely backward and forward and round and round). I had only just heard of pendulums at this early stage of my development. I had come to know about many tools with which to work during this time, and I was excited to try them all. So, as I held the pendulum over the map, I made sure it was still, no swinging at all. I knew that by asking specific questions whose answers I knew, I would be able to determine which direction indicated a yes answer and which indicated a no answer. First, I asked if my name was Rebecca; the pendulum swung back and forth - no. Just to make sure, I asked if I was 100 years old; the pendulum swung back and forth - no again. Finally, I asked if I was a girl and the pendulum swung round and round - yes! Now I was ready! Hovering the pendulum over places on the map, making sure always that the pendulum was totally still, I asked Chung Yoi, "Did you live here?" Over and over, the pendulum swung up and down for no. Finally, as I reached Thailand, the pendulum swung round and round for yes. Yippee, at last, I thought!

As I held the pendulum, however, it also swung up and down for no. Hmmm... I didn't understand that at all. As there had been a complete no for every other location, I had to assume that Thailand was both yes and no. Not at all clear, I left it there.

A few weeks later, I was walking through town and had an overwhelming urge to go into a charity shop. Once there, I was drawn to the old film and book section. I felt quite excited, as if I knew I would find something really good there. Just as I started to look, without even thinking I picked up film *The King and I*. Looking at the pictures on the cover, I noticed that all the people looked like my Chung Yoi. They even had buns on the tops of their heads, just like he did in my drawing! How wonderful is that, I thought. As I read the story of the film on the back, the word that jumped out at me was SIAM. That is where the story takes place (the musical is based upon a true story). Of course I bought the film. At home, I typed Siam into my computer and learned that Thailand was once called Siam, only the name had been changed in this century.

I've loved *The King and I* from childhood, and I have watched it a thousand times since this discovery, as doing so makes me feel very close to Chung Yoi. This, I believed, was the link. Finding that movie was Chung Yoi's way of helping me discover where he had lived when he last had a life on this Earth. So yes, it was Thailand and no, it wasn't Thailand. It was Siam. This answer was perfect and even today I am amazed at how clever it was of Chung Yoi to use this method to help me understand his true origins.

I then heard about a practice that if you had described me just a year previous I would have run for the hills and in double quick time. Yet now I was all excitement and anticipation. The practice was as follows. Sit in a dark room with just a candle to your side - either side, it makes no difference (although I like my right side best). Then look into a mirror and fix your eyes on a particular spot on your face, I was told your nose is a good place. As I stared at my nose in the mirror, my face started to change shape. It looked a little weird, with dark circles under my eyes. I was staring at my nose the whole time, yet I could still see the changes. At one point I looked a little dead - my face had turned grey and sunken, with the start of another face appearing atop mine. Together with the dark circles, I resembled a zombie more than my natural self. I wasn't frightened at all, however, as I automatically knew this transformation was a part of the process. Indeed, I felt a lovely sense of excitement, and had a sense of energy moving around me in waves. It was beautiful, and I knew the sensation was as real as the candle's flame beside me; it even danced to the same rhythm as the energy. The more intense the waves felt, the faster the flame flickered, as if they were corresponding. That in itself was wonderful to see and feel.

This practice took a lot of patience, as the more my face changed the more I wanted to study it. I wanted to stop focusing on my nose and look at my whole face, but of course as soon as I did the changes instantly disappeared. This may have been good, as I had to learn to stay focused on my nose no matter what happened to the bigger picture before me. Once I grasped this, the process was much easier. Sometimes my face changed so much I could see Chung Yoi over my entire face. It was amazing. One time, I stared so much that the mirror in front of me went completely black. Wow, this was new. There I was, looking at myself in the mirror only there was no reflection at all, not a jot, all was blackness. And from this blackness, independent of me and my features, came the face of my guide all on his own in the darkness, just him in all of his glory. I burst into tears at this, feeling that finally I knew him. I knew him as I knew my own self, he was that familiar to me. The feelings I experienced at this realization are difficult to describe. My guide felt like home to me, intensely nostalgic. I felt safe. What was even more remarkable was that Chung Yoi's face was the exact same as I had drawn it all those months ago in the art class.

Later I would practice this method of seeing with my friend Nikki. I would sit in front of the mirror and she would sit a little farther back from me. Often, we both saw my guide in the mirror at the same time. Then we would swap places and I would see in the mirror for her. Nikki loved my Chung Yoi, and often said, "Oh, he's lovely Deb. He's really handsome." This always made me laugh.

Months later I had a reading with a well-known teacher medium who said, "Your guide is here now." I've always been a little sceptical when it comes to people giving me guides, as I am never sure if I can I trust them. But this brilliant man went on: "He says he is your man from the east, and he tells me you have seen his face." Well I nearly fell off my chair! What good evidence for me. I was over the moon, thinking, "Yes!" My Chung Yoi let me know in no uncertain terms that he was definitely my guide. I had drawn him, named him, seen him in the mirror, and learnt the meaning of his name and where he had lived on Earth. And now he had been verified to me via a wonderfully respected medium. My journey to get to know my first guide was complete. What more could I have wished for?

I was very content with Chung Yoi for a long while, and had no need to look for any other guides. I sat in the power every day for between one and two and half hours. As stated above, sitting in the power is where you sit and quiet your mind so that it becomes void of thoughts. In this way, you become much more aware of your spiritual self and of those that guide you, which enables you to then communicate on a level above thought. In this level of communication, you are more open to the influence of spirit. To me this is different from a meditation as there is no visualization to follow, no planned out journey to imagine.

Generally, when sitting in power, I didn't see anything, sometimes I just felt. I believe everyone's experiences with sitting in the power are different. When I initially sat in the power, I knew Chung Yoi was there with me, as the energy that he enveloped me with had become as familiar to me as a hug from my mother. Once I had reached the developmental stage where he could influence my mind more, there were many times whilst sitting together that Chung Yoi took me on journeys to see his land. These journeys were as clear as if a colour movie was being played in my mind. It is important to note that this is very rare for me, as I am a person who does not visualize very well.

Every now and then, as I sat in the power with Chung Yoi, I had a different feeling come over me, as if the left side of my face and head had become numb or closed off if you like. I felt this conceptually rather than literally. I thought it might be an exercise in my development, as if my guide was helping me to strengthen my right brain by closing off the left side. To this day I imagine this to be true, but I thought at the time there might have been another reason for it as well. I will explain.

A few months later, I had another reading with the same gentleman (I had been taking a course with him). In this reading, he mentioned that I had another guide. Humph, I thought, I don't want another guide. I want Chung Yoi. In my naivety I believed at the time that you could only have one guide. My reader assured me of the contrary. Then he said I had an Egyptian princess with me and that she was a scribe. I had no idea what a scribe was, nor was I sure I trusted the reader. Well, I thought, I won't take this new guide on board until I have some proof that she is with me. My hesitation was due in part to my belief that being given a guide does not automatically mean the person doing the giving is right. Also, I was comfortable with Chung Yoi and wanted to keep it that way.

Not even a week later, I got the same urge to go into a charity or thrift shop. Why charity shops, I don't to this day know. Perhaps I am drawn to them because that is where you can pick up all sorts of old and different things. As I walked in, straight ahead of me was the biggest bust of Nefertiti I had ever seen. She was green and gold and stood at least 2_ feet high. As you may know, Nefertiti was an Egyptian Queen and Tutankhamen's probable mother (history is not sure if it was her or another wife of the King of Egypt that bore Tut). Of course, I was quite shocked. When in the world would a big bust of Nefertiti just present itself to you? Convinced, I brought her home with me and accepted that yes I did have an Egyptian guide.

I am not suggesting, however, that it is Nefertiti who is my guide, though how wonderful would that be? The medium said only that my guide was a princess, and Nefertiti was never a princess, but had been a Queen. Still, it is said that Nefertiti was blind in her left eye, and the thought briefly crossed my mind that maybe that is why I felt that one side of my face was shut off whilst sitting in the power. I include this information here, as I believe that we all need to remain levelheaded when it comes to identifying our guides. Yes, it would be lovely to have a famous guide, but truthfully the odds are really against such an occurrence. I could have grown the thought and "made" Nefertiti my guide, but what purpose would that serve? I would only do such a thing if I had the urge to elevate myself, to grow my ego. Instead, I quickly came to my senses. I believe that having the closed off sensation on the left side of my face/brain is how I originally said it was: an experience meant to help the right side of my brain become more active.

What we must remember is that we are already important, just as important even as the so-called "famous" guides. Earthly fame has no value in the spirit world - please remember that. If you feel that you have a guide well known for the life lived here on Earth, then please do all of the research needed to confirm this. Produce credible evidence to the fact that no one can dispute. This is important because there are already millions of people who feel that the work mediums do is the stuff of make believe. One of our jobs is to help critics recognize that there is life after life. When there are mediums running around claiming Elvis Presley is their guide, it does no favours to our cause or our credibility. Even if you are right and the spirit who was Elvis Presley has decided to be your guide, please, please unless, as I say, you have undeniable proof, it may be wise to discern just who needs to know that information.

I have never found out the name of my lovely Egyptian lady, though I'm sure if I performed the same seeing practice as I did with Chung Yoi I would be able to gain this information. Truthfully, I have always called her Nefi and I believe she finds this cute. She lets me know that knowing her real name is not so important and that, as she likes my nickname for her, there is no real reason to discover more. Furthermore, I have found that I am at a place where having to know every detail about my guides is not a priority, maybe because I feel such love from them. Or maybe it is enough that they have both shown me in evidential ways that they are with me. I do not need any more proof than that; I am quite content.

Chapter 33
Me and My Guides

Keeping notes is a great way of recognizing your progress. Use this space to journal about your growing relationship with your guides.

Date:
Progress notes:

Date:
Progress notes:

Date:
Progress notes:

Date:
Progress notes:

Date:
Progress notes:

Date:
Progress notes:

Date:
Progress notes:

Date:
Progress notes:

Date:
Progress notes:

Date:
Progress notes:

Chapter 34
Using Symbols Within Mediumship

You believe in God? Believe also in your imagination.
Neville Goddard 1905 – 1972

Ah, symbols; they are balm to your mediumship as is the flower to the bee! Working with symbols in your work is like the military using Morse code to transmit accurate information: the numbers and letters typed mean exactly what they mean with no room for misinterpretation.

So it is with your mediumistic symbols, and the best thing is YOU decide what they will be, no one else does the choosing. Some people work this way naturally. Their minds are geared, if you like, to this method of remembering. I see using symbols as a way of thinking by association, where one thing stands for this, and another thing stands for that. For some of us, however, this is not a natural process; we may need to bring in a structured method to make symbols a part of our work.

Take me for instance, I associate well with numbers, but I am not so natural with objects. I believe this is because objects have to be visualized in order to work and visualization is not a strong point of mine. At the start of my development, my guides actually forced a few symbols into my mediumship to get me to recognize them. That is not a pleasant way to go about such a discovery, as it may take a good number of readings and a good number of nos from clients for the penny to drop.

Here is an example of how this happened to me. Out of the blue one day, the name "Wendy" started coming to me during readings. As with any other name, I gave it to the recipient. Imagine, then, my confusion when the recipient said, "No." I could only assume the recipient (also known as the sitter) would eventually get the name by way of remembering someone. Now this went on for quite a while. I received the name whilst doing private readings but also while in demonstrations. Soon, the name came up more and more often. Frustrated, I sat down one day and asked myself, "Why do I keep getting the name Wendy when it always turns out to be wrong?" That's when I finally asked myself, "What does the name mean to me?" Well the ONLY Wendy I had ever known was a child from next door as I was growing up. So, Wendy was a neighbour. The next time I had the thought of Wendy, I said to my recipient, "You must have had a neighbour recently pass over." The answer was "yes." Aha! I'd cracked the mystery. Now, every time I "hear" the name Wendy I know that it means that the recipient has a neighbour that has passed away.

After a while, whenever I heard the name Wendy I also got the imaginary feeling that someone was standing off to my right. Now, when I do not feel that presence, I know that I have to say the name Wendy specifically, instead of assuming it is that of a neighbour. You see, as my Paul always says, "Mediumship is like an imaginary pantomime that goes on in your mind." I believe that my guides chose this name/symbol specifically. Because I moved around so much in my life, especially in my childhood, I never really became long-term friends with my neighbours. For others, however, they are like family. Without this gentle nudge or reminder, I would have missed an important "relative" to bring through to be remembered.

In order to work with symbols efficiently, you need to find what best resonates with you. It is no good making up elaborate symbols that mean nothing, as you will then struggle to remember what they stand for. Symbols MUST come from your life, as their efficiency will ALWAYS come down to what they mean to you. Not to spirit, not to the recipient, but to you! Symbols work on the same lines as word association. Your symbols must be objects or words that cause the same instant reaction each time they enter your mind.

The best way to make your list is to "make up" symbols off the top of your head. Write a list of objects and then write what they mean to you. From then on, every time you work and "see" or "hear" one of your symbols, you will know exactly what it means. This is your spiritual shorthand, your very own spiritual language. It will make your life and the life of your guides so much easier. Symbols also help your communicators, as they will then know exactly what you need in order to get their evidence across. One of the benefits of this method is that it will be difficult to get information wrong within your evidence.

Of course, your evidence should grow all the time and therefore your list should grow with it. There will always be surprises to what evidence they would like you to bring through for them, so never become complacent. Always push and strive for more. Your list will also eliminate a lot of nervousness, as one of the main reasons nerves get the better of us is that we have to stand up in front of an audience with nothing. We cannot write our evidence down before we stand up, as we don't know who is going to come through. We cannot research or rehearse, but at least with symbols you have structure to your work. At least as much structure as one can have whilst doing this work.

Using symbols is not just about making the job easier for everyone involved, however. The main reason it improves our work is that it also gives us the opportunity to get greater evidence! The longer your list, the more evidence spirit can drop into your thoughts and mind's eye without you needing to puzzle out the evidence before giving the information to your recipient. I believe ninety percent of the nos received within a demonstration or one to one sitting are not really nos, but an indication that the medium has misinterpreted the information given by the communicator. That is yet another benefit to using symbols within your work.

What I especially adore, however, is what happens after you make your list. There you are in full flow whilst working when suddenly you see one of your symbols in your mind's eye. You go with it and give the recipient what it is you have associated with that object/word. How great when the recipient says yes, and that you are correct. This will happen time and time again within the reading. Once you've finished, the feeling of happiness and gratitude is indescribable. That is when you know for sure that spirit has seen your list! This in turn makes you feel so much closer to your guides, like you are members of a team or best friends. A huge amount of trust is then gained in your relationship, which is an essential key to becoming a fantastic medium: good at your job, and worthy of the title "Bringer of Peace."

Chapter 35
Me and My Symbols

As with personal affirmations, guides, goals, and most other aspects of your mediumship, your symbols and their importance will change over time. Use this space to record your symbols and what each symbol means to you.

Date:
My Symbols:

Date:
My Symbols:

Date:
My Symbols:

Chapter 36
Meditation and Mediumship

Meditation is the tongue of the soul and the language of the spirit.
Jeremy Taylor 1613 - 1667

There are so many views on meditation and its purposes, and it is indeed a very brood subject. As we are only covering intuition, mediumship, and psychic ability, it's best that we stay as close as we can to those categories.

I call meditation "having time for my spiritual space," whilst Debs will say "sitting in the power." I'm afraid I just don't have the patience Debs has, so to dedicate a whole hour or so it is just too much for me. Instead, I average about fifteen to twenty minutes five mornings a week.

I spent much of the first year of my initiation going from one development circle to another, experiencing many different styles of meditation, each with its own justification and an owner to defend its necessity for spiritual growth. Meditating is very individual. When asked today what is the best method, I always say, "Do what's good for you with no pressure."

In developing your own practice, ask yourself the following questions. Why do I meditate? What are my goals? Am I searching for an experience or simply some quiet time? What are my purposes in regard to work? Do I want to feel closer to those I work with in spirit, such as guides or loved ones?

Truthfully I feel there are no hard or fast rules to meditating. Do what you feel is good for you. Don't get bogged down with repeating rituals to start. Some people feel they need to say a prayer or chant words of protection. I find this is unnecessary. Though I do say a few words to my guides when starting, as that is my way of feeling who I am working with and at what intensity, my intention is never to protect myself or ask for a blessing in any way. I have been meditating for many years now and have never experienced anything negative, threatening or evil in any way.

Another concern is where to meditate. Again, there are many theories on what is best, but I sit mostly on my own in the comforts of my living room, with no special position or chair, just our family couch. I usually meditate five mornings a week but this is only because my job and schedule allow for it. Do I need to meditate five days each week? No. My practice was just as fulfilling five years ago when I only had time to meditate once a week. Similarly, I feel you can get as much out of a ten-minute meditation as you can from an hour. Nor do I have specific rules and/or a set time. If I only meditate for ten minutes, then that's all I need that day. If it's twenty minutes the next, then it's twenty minutes. I meditate with no expectations other than spending time with those I work with from spirit, my guides.

I believe there have always been unfair expectations placed upon novices beginning meditation. This is often due to the expectations or claimed results of others. Firstly, what you experience and the perception of your experience will be very different from the next person. This is also true for the level of realism felt within the meditation. Let's not kid ourselves, any person describing his/her experiences in meditation has the potential to exaggerate, and how can we prove otherwise. That's not to say this is the case for everybody, but in my experience it is true for 50 to 60 percent of those I have spoken to over the years. But who's to say my view is correct? After all, each person has his/her own interpretation.

Regardless of your approach, you should always respect your meditations and the teachings behind them by keeping them as real and honest as you can. This means not letting your ego take over. This will also apply to your psychic development. Generally, those who exaggerate their meditation experiences also exaggerate their ability to use mediumship. In my view your meditations are your testing ground for spirit, a place where they can assess your strengths and weaknesses, test how visual and how sensitive you can be. A meditative place is an experience that should remain personal; you are developing your intuition not moving mountains.

So how will you know if your guides are with you? Allow your imagination (or for the spiritually politically correct person, your mind's eye) to see them. It's as simple as that. There's no big BANG. During meditation, see the visualization purely in your trusted thoughts; believe it's happening without letting your imaginative overdrive take over what you are experiencing. This may take practice. If you're looking for guides, relax and understand that it may take a few goes before you see a clear picture.

When meditating, I generally find a quiet spot (my living room at 6:00am). The intensity of my meditations varies from day to day. This is something again that people get hung up on, asking themselves whether they have gone deep enough. It is important in meditating to clear your mind. Giving this, or any other issue, too much thought before or during your meditation just puts pressure on you and the whole process. I sometimes go very deep into my meditation, although that is something I don't insist upon. On other days, I remain very aware of where I am and what noises are around me. When this happens, I don't feel I've reached a true meditative state during my session. In the early days, this frustrated me to the point of my not being able to meditate at all. Don't go there; meditation is a moving process; you have to remain flexible and maintain trust in order to benefit from the practice. There have been times when I've said to myself, "Well what was the point of giving the time to this morning's session." I mean, I was aware of every minute and did not shift my energy or calm my thoughts in any way, or I spent much of the time thinking about the day ahead. What I've learned to recognize is that although my mind is very alert, my body is not. I still experience that heavy, relaxed feeling I get when my meditations go well.

Remember your meditations are there to complement your mediumship not be your mediumship. Together, they pair up like a good relationship - both very much have their own personalities and like to be a little independent, but they are always supportive of one other.

Finally, expecting duplicate experiences will become a disappointment. Don't try too hard to return to the same meditation as a previous session. Do what's right for you, don't judge your experiences by others, and you'll do well.

Chapter 37
Sensitivity and Mediumship

In the depths of your hopes and desires, lies your silent knowledge of the beyond, and like seeds dreaming beneath the snow, your heart dreams of spring. Trust the dreams, for in them is hidden the gate to eternity.
                                    Kahlil Gibran 1883 – 1931

These days a lot of focus is put on the sensitivity of a medium's work, which generally relates to how well the client or audience feels you worked at the time. For instance, how accurate was the evidence given? Was it generic or very detailed? How many people in the audience received a message? And so on. I have become more and more sensitive over the years. It's strange - even now that I am more experienced I still get caught off-guard when my emotions become overwhelming. And I'm not talking only about mediumship sensitivity, but also my personal sensitivity.

As I write this piece Debs and I are coming to the end of a fairly difficult day as husband and wife. I found myself panicking over the business in ways that are not really necessary - and was unable to simply agree with Debs' approach and call it a day. I knew she was right, as we had just worked for sixteen hours straight, but I still felt my heightened emotions were justified, otherwise I would not have been experiencing them. Should I have said, "I'm sorry"? Was I waiting for Debs to fill the gaps in my own confidence? Why else would I have needed reassurance that she can manage all she says she can with the Accolade workload? Was I just being damn selfish? Is it possible that increased sensitivity also exposes my stubborn steak more than usual? Life as a sensitive can be tough you know.

Sensitivity is a trait that we tend to forget about whilst developing our mediumistic abilities, but the truth is, the more evolved your mediumship, the more sensitive you will become. Even knowing this, I still sometimes find myself surprised at the waves of emotions that come over me - whether at home or going about my daily life. I am especially susceptible to these when discussing personal matters, even those that at one time had little effect on my emotions. It's in those moments that you have to stop and take stock of your reactions, acknowledging how strong your emotions are running. Think about what you are feeling and why. Most importantly, learn to recognize that your increased emotional sensitivity is a complement to your mediumship sensitivity.

Yes, this is true! Sensitivity grows from the inside out, not from the outside in. You have to become sensitive as a being in order to become sensitive spiritually. You may think, "What a thorn in the side." Right? But remember the tool is only as good as the material it's made from, and you are the tool.

Each time you dip into the toolbox of your mediumship, or any other spiritual activity for that matter, you are working a muscle the same as working on your abs when doing sit-ups. This muscle becomes stronger within your mediumship, just as working your abs increases your midsection. So, the next time you find yourself slipping out of character and getting weepy at a sad ending to your favourite television program, resist the urge to label your newfound emotion as "depression," or to exaggerate and put it to some negative entity shadowing you. Instead, stop and think: you made this happen the moment you made a conscious decision to develop your mediumship.

As an emotional being there are many elements to the construction of each and every reaction you have in life. As your mediumship grows stronger, so will your senses. This is to complement the need for sensitivity on all levels. For example, why do I find myself on an emotional downer after a few cocktails? Alcohol is a depressant, of course, but I've never had this problem before. Truth is, although I was able to cope with a certain amount at one time in my life, alcohol has now become too harsh for my tingling, ever-growing sensitive body. That's not to say I don't have a cocktail or two when I'm not working. After all I am a full-blooded Welshman and having a few beers is part of our culture! But I have learnt to recognize the blue feeling I get after a night out with Debs and the family.

Should you become aware of similar feelings, my advice is this: don't get bogged down by negative thoughts. Accept the responsibility of what it is you are changing within your system. Recognize that you are opening sensitive vessels within your being that have been waiting many years to be reborn or to be exercised for strength. You may feel like a pincushion, reacting to the tiniest of everyday upsets, or you may feel overjoyed by the smallest of ventures. Whatever your reactions, always see them as a positive and remember, the more sensitive you become as a human being the stronger your mediumship.

Chapter 38
Teacher Mediums: The Blind Teaching the Blind

Any fool can make something complicated. It takes a genius to make it simple.
                                                           Woody Guthrie

Globally, we are a society that demands everything instantly. And why not, we certainly have the technology and networks to support this desire. In turn, technology has made our world such a small place, allowing our wonderful species the freedom to travel the globe without even needing to leave our homes.

How do we weigh whether this is a good or bad change? That comes down to personal preference or experience, I believe. I myself find it hard to decide. I see my two daughters preferring to play on their laptops all day to getting outdoors during their free time. I agree that our fear of something unthinkable happening to our children whilst they are outside playing has come to the forefront, rather than remaining the distant concern it was for my parents, but must that mean that they should miss out on the life experiences their predecessors experienced? What is the benefit in favouring the cyber-experience of making friends through online social networks? It seems to me that reliance on such networking robs our younger generation of the life knowledge that comes from having contact with a variety of different personalities in their truest sense; getting to know the very essence of another person is only possible when time is spent together in person, not through the cables of internet social communities.

You see, my thought is that we are built to carry many forms of emotions, such as sympathy, empathy, respect, and tolerance, which in turn help us experience and become more in tune to our own sensitivity. How then will my two little girls experience and develop this needed range of emotions if they have not done the practical work to support them. The advancement of technology, while beneficial in some ways, robs those who rely on it too heavily of their natural ability to use their senses. This is due to the displacement of our natural habitat - trying to grasp experiences through a computer screen rather than actually living them ourselves.

Some three to four decades ago, experience ruled over knowledge. Here in the UK it was commonplace for young adults to leave school as early as possible. Have things improved over that time? Yes of course. My eldest daughter has had no professional training on computers, but despite that, and despite being only at the complicated age of eleven, she whizzes around the computer leaving me to shame. We have shifted, becoming a world of knowledge, a fact that is heightened by our ability to find any data we need on the internet. But are we still a world of experience? I fear not.

What am I getting at? The UK has thousands of tradespeople who are fully qualified yet cannot get employment due to a lack of experience in their chosen fields. This is mainly due to our demands as customers. Let's face it, would you have a hairstylist do your hair knowing it was his/her first time out of training? Or have a dentist pull your tooth if his/her only experience was in the training laboratory?

What has this debate to do with mediumship? For one thing, we have seen an increase in untrained, no-experience-necessary teaching mediums. In addition, many countries are adopting a system where no licensing is needed to teach mediumship, leaving the door wide open for the "I can do it but never have done it" teacher mediums. How can they even use the title teacher? I will let you be the judge of that one.

So what makes for a no experience teacher medium? Well here goes, it's time to stick my neck out. They are individuals who have done a few church demonstrations, maybe a handful of one to one readings and have attended a workshop or two. This seems sufficient and acceptable for up and coming mediums who then go to such teachers for training. Why? I get so confused by this. Which brings me back to our earlier discussion. When we go to any business for service, do we not search for the best and most experienced professionals we can find? We all want value for money, but that should never be at the detriment of quality.

It's crazy that future mediums are attending workshops all over the world led by teachers they expect to look up to and trust, yet who have very little or no experience. The worst cases are those who teach work they haven't the courage to do themselves. You know who they are!

There are many independent and spiritual establishments working hard to clean up and regulate this grey area, and doing a great job, but it's like trying to empty a bucket of water using a thimble whilst it is being refilled with a pint glass. As you can imagine, we have our work cut out for us.

I propose we take a stand and say we are no longer happy with no-experience teacher mediums. If we do not, their field will continue to grow by the day, populated by individuals trying to make a quick buck whilst doing nothing more than flexing their egos. It's easy to be a big fish in a little pond, as they say. And whilst I fully understand that the experience gained from teaching helps improve one's skills (and we all have to start our teaching career at some point), surely we should expect at least a competent level of experience in order to begin. I personally don't believe a handful of demonstrations and a few one to one readings come close to providing such qualification. How can anyone build their own teaching methods and material after carrying out a few short appointments? It's impossible.

Fortunately, there is no need to accept this as the norm. There are plenty of qualified instructors out there. Accolade Academy, The Arthur Findley Collage and many other reputable venues around the world employ fine, experienced professional teaching mediums to satisfy our needs. Accolade and many other spiritual institutions have also established teacher-training programs. You may think I am only looking to plug my own business, but let's face it, the days of relying solely on Dad to teach you to drive (and often sharing his bad driving habits) are long gone.

I suggest that before you put your mediumship and your hard earned money into another workshop, ask questions. Find out the teacher's level of experience. Is he/she still working publically on a regular basis in the areas to be taught? If so, at what level - professional or occasional? You might be shocked to find out that you hold more experience than the teacher.

Chapter 39

The (Sometimes Crazy) Ambassadors of Mediumship

Do not fear to be eccentric in opinion, for every opinion now accepted was once eccentric.

Bertrand Russell

In travelling, Debs and I hear many crazy stories, theories and opinions voiced by self-acclaimed, experienced spiritual workers all over the world. Here are a few of our favourites:

• A student once asked me if it was possible to steal another person's guide, as she had just been told that she needed to hang on tight to hers, as someone might just steal it during meditation.

• Another student stated that a professional teaching medium had advised him, "Your mediumship will be better if you can say something to a recipient that will upset the audience and get them angry just before you make your first link." Apparently, it was this professional's opinion that such upset helps to lift the audience's energy vibration.

• Sitting in circle, a working medium once said she felt she had Big Bird (from Sesame Street) with her from spirit.

• Debs was once approached by a professional working medium who advised her that if she (the medium) did not deliver the message she had from spirit to Debs then she (the medium) would fall physically ill herself (as spirit would impress an illness on her for not delivering the message). Her message was that Debs was in the early stages of cancer - which was hugely incorrect! The word therapy springs to mind.

• A distraught spiritualist church member once sought advice from a senior church member because she believed she had run over a spirit rabbit on the way to church that evening. The senior member advised her that from his experience it was not a spirit rabbit but probably one of her own guides that she a run down in the car.

• During a one to one reading in the USA, a client claimed that the universe had been trying to kill her in a car accident every year on her birthday.

Let's keep it real folks!

Chapter 40

Do We Need Protection?

Seeing the small is called clarity. Keeping flexible is called strength. Using the shining radiance you enter the light, where no harm can come to you. This is called enlightenment.
                                                            Lao Tzu 600BC

I have often been asked if I seek spiritual protection before I begin a reading or while I am giving evidential mediumship. I answer, "Absolutely not." I'm sorry to disappoint any obsessive-compulsive psychic mediums out there - yes, I said it, OCD is rife in our movement. I have heard so many experienced mediums tell students that they must repeat some ritual or chant or prayer over and over in order to be in a spiritually safe place. I have no wish to offend those who have been clinically diagnosed with this disorder, but rather the mediumistic predecessors who leave complicated, deeply instilled messes for forward-thinking mediums to clean up.

Aside from the word no, PROTECTION has to be the most negative word used in mediumship - a movement that is supposed to be known for its positive, loving nature. Not that I wish to get political in any way, as this is not what this book is about, but come on people, it's time to get real about this!

In our society, the word protect generally indicates a sense of vulnerability. Therefore, to feel the need to visualize a shield of protection can only subconsciously recall a host of underlying fears. Such fears can centre on current life challenges or those from the past. Perhaps you had very strict or demanding parents, or experienced physical discipline from those you looked up to during your childhood, which left you feeling a need to protect yourself in one way or another. We all have emotional triggers that are awakened by positive and negative starters. The words protect and protection are negative starters for any one of your emotional triggers. The resulting fear can be a complete self-destruction of your confidence on many levels, as it removes any newly built self-authorization that you have assumed over your mediumship. This authority is needed to strengthen your personality as part of the confidence building process of your mediumship development.

When I first started in this business, I followed the self-claimed ranking officers in our loving movement, believing for a very short time that if those with experience said we needed to visualize a layer of spiritual protection then it must be true. But each time I tried, it just did not sit well. I have never asked for protection in my life before, and doing so then seemed so alien to my personality. It also brought an unnecessary nervousness or mystic feeling to my new loving job that I was not prepared to adopt. By that, I mean the same kind of mystic feeling you experienced when as a child you watched a scary movie and then had to hide under the blankets in order to feel safe. Feeling this nervousness, I kept thinking, "Am I not working in what is claimed to be one of the most loving movements we can ever experience? Why would I need to protect my being or aura from spiritual attack?"

I have no doubt there are many who disagree with me on this, and hey, that's fine. Freedom of choice as they say. But here's a thought: many of our most respected authors and spiritual leaders often assert that our universal thoughts and perceptions are what make our reality. In other words, WE ARE WHAT WE THINK! Now we've opened a whole new can of worms! If we are what we think, then are we, with such exaggerations, not making an issue out of nothing? Where did this fear come from? Did it start with an overzealous spiritual person claiming that a negative entityhad threatened his or her wellbeing? Wherever it began, there has ever since been a faction of our community that insists that in order to practice your evidential mediumship in a safe manner, it is best to ask for protection. My question is, where are those individuals who have been threatened or attacked by the claimed negative spirits whilst working with their mediumship? What true physical evidence do they have of such an occurrence, and was it on the scale claimed by those mediums? Believe me, I have heard so many stories, from those who were impressed with a feeling like cardiac arrest when working to others who suffered enforced illness from spirit. And the strangest thing of all is that there is never anyone around to witness these events at the time of their happening. I am very open-minded, but I for one don't share these thoughts or fears.

Let's look at this in a little more detail. Surely if a spirit could harm you in any way whilst you are giving evidential mediumship or having a blissful meditation, that spirit would have no conscience in doing so. Why stop at mere possession when it could do some real harm? Let's face it, the spirit has no worries of going to prison, so the sky's the limit, as they say. I for one have never seen any headlines in our local newspaper: "Person Murdered By Ghost In Park." Yet, I have heard so many stories whilst travelling, and, to be quite frank, have read similar tales in our advertising. It seems to me that some of our internationally acclaimed workers would do well to attend a few sessions of therapy rather than passing on faulty advice to novices who don't know better. This sounds a little harsh, I know, but sometimes the word "ego" comes to mind.

Years ago I asked myself, would I take a job where I felt the need to seek protection each day. I'm sorry, if I believed this were the case I would do something else for a living. Who would clock into a job where they felt the need to pray for protection from those working within their company before even setting foot onto the premises? No one I know. It is no different in our profession. I believe that I, like everyone else on this Earth, already have a trusted, natural source of protection. If I didn't I wouldn't have the courage to step outside each day, much less travel around the world with Accolade.

We have very powerful minds, and I'm sure that if I gave it enough thought and intention I could convince myself overnight that I had lost the ability to walk. Through their own power of mind many people have self-cured diseases that modern day medical doctors failed to conquer. It isn't hard to understand how some in our profession have come to fear spirits. Allowing oneself to hold the belief that we are vulnerable to negative spirits whilst working is a breeze for anyone whose imagination is in overdrive.

Like you and many others, I believe we have guides. Naturally, I have to rely on my imagination to a degree to hold this belief. And like most people in this movement, I also believe I am spirit and spirit is universe and universe is God, so I must ask myself - would my God wish me to come to any spiritual harm? Of course not.

We could go round in circles all day on this subject, so I will leave you with this thought: to get the absolute most out of what it is you love, you have to believe it loves you even more. How do we get to that place? By having complete trust in that love, and knowing it means us no harm.

Chapter 41
Global Spiritualism and the Phrase Psychic/Medium

I start with the premise that the function of leadership is to produce more leaders, not more followers.

Ralph Nader

When I think about mediumship as a spiritual movement and a business, I have to ask: Where is the phrase Psychic Medium headed in the world? Are we, as an industry, growing stronger, increasing public confidence and trust? Or are we, through our spiritual organizations, handing the press all they need to further disillusion the public and spread the idea that we are just an irrational bunch of people who feed off crazy ideas and claim to have powers reserved for the chosen or gifted?

It's only been eight years since I made the commitment to work fulltime as a medium, entering uncharted waters that have changed my life in a ways I never expected. I thought the world was strange enough before becoming a professional medium; boy was I in for a shock! It isn't my mediumship that has brought the strangest or weirdest experiences, however, but some of the people I've encountered within the Spiritualist religion - people claiming to be the forerunners and ambassadors of this wonderful movement.

Although Spiritualism is a global religion, it is in the minority as far as mainstream religions go, not only in terms of acceptance, but also in regard to rules and regulation. Whereas many religions have a single, main governing body, Spiritualism does not. Rather it is made up of a variety of congregations throughout the world, all with very different guidelines. What does not change, however, is that it is a religion that relies on mediums to provide one of the main sources of its income; the demonstrating of the mediumship portion of our Divine service is a main attraction for a large percentage of its public congregation and free will offerings.

Now why do I want to discuss religion when the focus of this book is mediumship? Well, there are thousands of individuals all over the world who are training to use their mediumship beneath the guidance of Spiritualist churches and independent spiritualist centres. Speaking from my own experience and the experience of thousands of individuals that Debs and I meet every year all over the world who trained using this service - developing one's mediumship in this sector is no less confusing than studying with the independent, no-experience-needed teacher mediums we discussed earlier in this book, many of whom have no part in the religion in any way. You see, many Spiritualist churches have no experienced professional mediums working on staff either full or part-time. Rather, they rely on mediums like Debs and me to make annual visits and offer training. In between those visits, they recruit volunteers - chosen from among the church committee, or from the most experienced (unpaid) mediums affiliated with the church - to fill in and offer training.

To my disappointment, I must say that their approach and methods used when teaching mediumship are often questionable, dated and too strictly controlled. For instance, many insist that students and/or church members will be vulnerable to negative spiritual attacks if they don't practice the teachings to the letter of the church.

I know there will be churches and centres that disagree with me on this one, as individually each organization likes to think they are giving the best training possible, directed with all the love, light and guidance that the spirit world has to offer. Perhaps I sound as if I am anti-Spiritualist, when in fact I am the complete opposite. I am a Spiritualist myself, not born into the religion but adopted in as part of my work as a professional medium. Debs and myself conduct many Divine services and other duties for the Spiritualist community all over the world, and we both hold Ministers' Certification. Did being a part of the Spiritualist church give me the knowledge or experience needed to grow my mediumship? The answer to that one has to be "No." Do I practice this religion in or through my teachings? No. Too often the church's rules and regulations are not for the benefit of your mediumship, but for the benefit of the committees' ego. Many church leaders have the belief that no student can or should supersede, becoming in any way a better medium. I have seen this attitude many times in many establishments all over the world.

Debs and I love what we do for a living and give much of our free time to improving the public profile of mediumship as well as raising awareness of the Spiritualist religion that relies on mediumship as part of its service to congregations. I like to think I am a levelheaded person, but by damn my patience has been tested, sometimes to the point that I've questioned my own sanity. Many Spiritualist leaders battle progress in their churches due to their own insecurities, often about their ability to use their mediumship. Such leaders insist that their complicated and somewhat unbelievable teachings are the only way forward, leaving students, or what these leaders call "fledglings" (a word I resent), not knowing which way to turn. I have seen and heard senior church mediums all over the world exaggerate experiences they claim occurred because of spirit. Some say they receive messages from other church members or students' guides whilst in some kind of meditative state in class. These messages most often offer guidance insisting students follow the church teacher medium's every order. I mean, this is not education; it's control, nothing more. I have yet to meet anybody other than me who can link to my guides. After all, they are my guides. I have seen students shaking with nerves and fear over something as petty as not holding the correct stance when delivering mediumship from the church rostrum. This, they've been told, can attract negative spiritual energy, as they are leaving themselves open to attack. And this comes from the church advisory! It's just insane.

We in the movement then wonder why it is the press has such an easy time making us look like a bunch of school children playing imaginary games in the playground.

Has Spiritualism lost its desire for realism in our shared movement? Are we afraid that eliminating the exaggerations and mysticism would leave us with no spiritual mediumship or psychic vocabulary? Simply put, there is a lack of evidential proof to back what some church mediums claim to see, feel, and hear when working for Spirit in any fashion. And because members rarely challenge their claims, for fear of being expelled from the church, it's become a free for all. I have spent much of my free time with senior church mediums who want to discuss and share their spiritual experiences. They often ask my advice, looking for an explanation for things they claim came from spirit whilst they were working with their mediumship. On many occasions I have had to think long and hard before replying, wanting to be as tactful as I possibly can without suggesting the individual may need to seek therapy.

Please know this complaint is not aimed at all hard-working, platform Spiritualist mediums. Nor do I refer to the many great, intentional churches and centres scattered around the globe that strive to prove their words and teach with the view of the betterment of their students. Rather than being ruled by their egos, such churches and individuals understand that this leads to a greater quality of mediumship for the church, looking always to push fast-forward and maintain a fresh, believable approach that complements the modern student.

Here at Accolade, we can proudly say we have worked in many such churches. If you look carefully, you will find them yourself. The secret to locating a reliable church is to look for certain qualities: a good church will happily nurse your development, not seeking to control it or you. Such a church will always want you to experience more than what they have to offer. In your search, don't be manipulated into anything other than what you feel is good for you. Yes, all churches have their own regulations and procedures, but you will be pleasantly surprised to learn that some of these are for your benefit, not theirs.

I finish this with a heartfelt plea to all who are at all involved in Spiritualism or use their psychic/mediumship in any way: please, keep it real. We have a responsibility to ensure our field is believable. Let's stop feeding the press. We are not children but adults claiming the desire to help others, so let's act like adults.

Keep these tips in mind and you will do well; this I speak from repeated personal experience.

Chapter 42
My Goals

Making a list of your goals is vital to sustaining focus and to keeping a positive momentum in your career. Again, these will change over time. Periodically take stock; review your goals and copy these pages as needed.

Use this space to record your goals.

Date:
Immediate Goals:

Six Months from Now:

Twelve Months from Now:

18 Months from Now:

24 Months from Now:

36 Months from Now:

Chapter 43
Recommended Reading

A truly good book teaches me better than to read it. I must soon lay it down, and commence living on its hint. What I began by reading, I must finish by acting.
                                                    Henry David Thoreau

Mediumship is not only a beautiful process; it is but a tiny part of a whole philosophy.

When I first began my journey through mediumship, travelling a maze of new feelings and thoughts and by the beauty of synchronicity, many a book came my way. Not just any books, but ones I could completely trust to help me get a greater understanding of the pieces in the puzzle that is the universal philosophy.

There are many different opinions as to the origins of the spirit and the reasons for its existence. I believe that it is very important to not only develop your mediumship, but to also educate yourself on subjects and theories pertinent to getting to know your own spirit. This practice will benefit your mediumship one thousand percent.

I believe that no one living on Earth, not even the great masters, has even a 1% grasp on the truth of this process called life. There are many different religions, and with them countless ideas from every angle imaginable. In order to form your own opinions, it is best to study as much as you can. I quite like Albert Einstein's theory, which simply put is this: "My religion consists of a humble admiration of the illimitable superior spirit who reveals himself in the slight details we are able to perceive with our frail and feeble mind." But I also have my own theory, which starts with one easy thought: for every question you have about the afterlife, think of the most loving answer possible and that will be your answer. No punishment, no rewards, all is love.

You see I do not believe there is one answer, one process, and one approach to this one question. I feel the true answers are so full of paradoxes that our human mind, no matter how advanced, no matter how spiritual, or how learned cannot possibly grasp them. I believe that there are those who get glimpses of a truth whilst in the physical body, glimpses earned by a life that yearns for truth. I also believe that these glimpses provide enough for us all to live "on Earth as it is in Heaven," if we so choose. It just takes discipline, not to obtain the glimpse, but to leave behind the old habits that blind us from that truth. I also believe this is the main goal, above all else, of the spirit that inhabits a body - to get to that truth with full consciousness, for the spirit to be fully present in the body and to allow the personality/ego to disappear behind it.

Mediumship for me not only reunites people with the precious people that they have lost, it at the same time cannot help but show the recipient his/her own immortality. Now dear readers, nothing, I repeat nothing, is a greater gift that you can ever give someone in this life. Therefore, go forth and let it be known - mediumship is never about the dead, it is always about and for the living!

In the first two years of what I like to call my awakening, I read everything I could get my hands on that dealt with the philosophy of life and what comes after. I had what I can only describe as a thirst for knowledge, one that I could not quench. After each book ended I would actually grieve for it, wishing that I could start again and gain the feelings of new hope all over again. These books brought me so much comfort, so much understanding. And so many of them, I realized, had helped me to remember rather than learn, as I would find myself nodding in agreement with most of what I read, feeling like I was at last putting words to what I already knew somewhere deep down inside, buried under the illusion of this surface life.

To help anyone on a similar journey, I have put together a list of the books that helped me along my path.

- *A little light on Ascension* – Diana Cooper
- *A New Earth: Awakening to Your Life's Purpose* – Eckhart Tolle
- *Ageless Body, Timeless Mind: The Quantum Alternative to Growing Old* – Deepak Chopra
- *Autobiography of Emma Hardinge Britten* – Emma Hardinge Britten; Margaret Wilkinson
- Conversations With God (Books 1, 2 and 3) - Neale Donald Walsch
- Destiny of Souls: New Case Studies of Life Between Lives – Michael Newton, PhD
- *Home Coming: Reclaiming and Championing Your Inner Child* – John Bradshaw
- *Journey of Souls: Case Studies of Life Between Lives* – Michael Newton, PhD
- *Many Lives, Many Masters* – Dr. Brian L. Weiss, M.D.
- *Messages from the Masters: Tapping into the Power of Love* – Brian Weiss, M.D.
- *On the Edge of the Etheric: Or Survival After Death Scientifically Explained* – Arthur Findlay
- *Synchrodestiny* – Deepak Chopra
- *The Celestine Prophecy* - James Redfield

- *The I that is We* – Richard Moss M.D.
- *The Power of Now: A Guide to Spiritual Enlightenment* – Eckhart Tolle
- *The Road Less Travelled: A New Psychology of Love, Traditional Values, and Spiritual Growth* – M. Scott Peck
- *The Rock of Truth* – Arthur Findlay
- *The Tenth Insight: Holding the Vision* – James Redfield
- *Three Magic Words: The Key to Power, Peace and Plenty* – Uell Stanley Anderson
- *Voices in my Ear: The Autobiography of a Medium* – Doris Stokes
- *What the Bleep Do We Know!?* (Film) – William Arntz; Betsy Chasse; Mark Vicente
- "You are gods": psalm 82-6, Gospel of St John 10-34 – Omraam Mikhael Aivanhov
- *You Can Heal your Life* – Louise L Hay

At one time or another all of the above books counted as my bible. There are countless others out there that will resonate with you. So go forth, dear reader and find your bibles.

To give you an idea of how such books can help you, not only your mediumship but with your awakening to yourself, your spirit, the whole philosophy behind our origins, our true home, our true self, of which mediumship is but a tiny part, I am including the following book review from one of Accolade's monthly newsletters.*

In Tune with the Infinite, Ralph Waldo Trine
(Published by G. Bell, London, 1965)
Book Review by Deborah Rees – Accolade Academy

Have you read The Secret? Have you read The Law of Attraction? Have you read the countless books on this subject that have been circulating in the last ten years or so? Great, that's brilliant, they are good books and one can learn a lot from them. Yet I hold in my hand another wonderful book, by

Ralph Waldo Trine, about the natural and spiritual laws that govern us. In Tune with the Infinite also discusses the idea that thoughts have energy that, for good or bad, determines our future. We are, Trine says, in control of our tomorrows as we chose what we pay attention to and think about. This gem was first published in... wait for it... 1899! 1899, you say? And I say, Oh My God, how has it taken us so long to pay attention to or even acknowledge such an idea?

Not only does he speak profoundly and eloquently about his subjects, Trine also discusses the process of death, instructing us not to mourn too greatly, as life is ever lasting. More important, he tells us, is the fact that communion with those departed from this form of life is THERE FOR ALL OF US!!! At last somebody said it, and they said it back in 1899. I take a bow to Mr. Trine. Here is an excerpt:

"And so far as the element of separation is concerned, he realizes that spiritual communion, whether between two persons in the body, or two persons, one in the body and one out of the body, is within reach for all. In the degree that the higher spiritual life is realized can there be this higher spiritual communion. (The degree of belief.)
The things that we open ourselves to always come to us. People in the olden times expected to see angels and they saw them, but there is no more reason why they should have seen them, than we should see them now, for the great laws governing all things are the same today as they were then" (124).

You see how, In just those short sentences, this genius spoke about life after death, telling us we can communicate not only with those passed over, but with guides and angels, and that how well we do this is up to us and our own belief in subject. This also touches upon the law of attraction, and reminds us that we have spiritual laws that allow for such communication.

Another excerpt:

> *"Within each one lies the cause of whatever comes to him. Each has it in his own hands to determine what comes. Everything in the visible, material world has its origin in the unseen, the spiritual, the thought world. This is the world of cause, the former is the world of effect. The nature of the effect is always in accordance with the nature of the cause. What one lives in his invisible, thought world he is continually actualizing in his visible material world. If he would have any conditions different in the latter he must make the necessary change in the former.*
>
> *A clear realization of this great fact would bring success to thousands of men and women who all about us now are in the depths of despair, it would bring health, abounding health and strength to thousands now diseased and suffering. It would bring peace and joy to thousands now unhappy and ill at ease (128-129).*

This has to be one of the best books I've read in recent years. Right here, we have many of today's greatest spiritual philosophies rolled into one book. I love it, and I highly recommend it. J

Happy reading, folks.

Other books from Capall Bann's range of 300+ titles:

Gift - Spiritual Wealth to Financial Wealth by Elizabeth Francis
This book delves into the realms of psychic phenomenon, knocking down the myths that stop people developing their abilities and providing step-by-step guides to help the reader along the path to becoming a professional psychic. *Gift* includes contacting and working with spirit, interpreting spiritual messages, unlocking and developing your psychic abilities and divining using tarot. In addition Gift contains experienced and practical advice on turning professional, from selecting courses and structuring sessions to operating as a small business, whether independent or working for an agency. ISBN 186163 322x £12.95

A Medium's Tale by Jenny Martin
A true story of one woman's spiritual journey in which she has to overcome many difficulties and challenges along the way. Yes, she wants to do something different with her life and in her search discovers an identity way beyond anything she had expected and begins a most incredible pathway which would surpass even the most vivid of imaginations. She faces prejudice, ignorance and sheer bloody mindedness but knows she is on a mission though does not know where it will all end. A rollercoaster of a story which will have you hanging on in disbelief but be warned, it's controversial and not for the faint-hearted either. Are you ready? ISBN 186163 3262 £11.95

Green Living, Sacred Life by Susan M. Phillips and Tye Jamie Coxston
Spiritual, money-saving and environmental all at the same time! From recycling tips to spiritual development this book is fun, interesting and enlightening to read. It is all about doing things to make you feel good, very simple relaxation to advanced meditation, breathing (incredibly something many people forget to do), gentle exercise and delicious recipes for all tastes including vegans and gluten free diets. Looking at the spiritual side, you need not be of any religion, and it does not matter if you are atheist or agnostic, you will find suggestions on developing your spirituality in ways that harm no one and nothing. The authors look at why we are trying to save the world giving honest reasons for the suggestions, this book is not what you should and must do; it is simply what the authors suggest and the whys and implications of such actions, fun with it, interesting facts and great ideas and recipes. This book is not a novel you have to read page by page, nor a book with lessons; you read what you want when you want. Have fun, saving the world. Increasing your awareness and spirituality, to make your living green and spirituality sacred, is not necessarily difficult; it can be fun and involve as many people as you want. ISBN 186163 3238   £15.95

FREE DETAILED CATALOGUE

Capall Bann is owned and run by people actively involved in many of the areas in which we publish. A detailed illustrated catalogue is available on request, SAE or International Postal Coupon appreciated. **Titles can be ordered direct from Capall Bann,** by post (cheque or PO with order), via our web site **www.capallbann.co.uk** using credit/debit card or Paypal, or from good bookshops and specialist outlets.

A Breath Behind Time, Terri Hector
A Soul is Born by Eleyna Williamson
Angels and Goddesses - Celtic Christianity & Paganism, M. Howard
The Art of Conversation With the Genius Loci, Barry Patterson
Arthur - The Legend Unveiled, C Johnson & E Lung
Astrology The Inner Eye - A Guide in Everyday Language, E Smith
Auguries and Omens - The Magical Lore of Birds, Yvonne Aburrow
Asyniur - Women's Mysteries in the Northern Tradition, S McGrath
Beginnings - Geomancy, Builder's Rites & Electional Astrology in the European Tradition, Nigel Pennick
Between Earth and Sky, Julia Day
The Book of Seidr, Runic John
Caer Sidhe - Celtic Astrology and Astronomy, Michael Bayley
Call of the Horned Piper, Nigel Jackson
Can't Sleep, Won't Sleep, Linda Louisa Dell
Carnival of the Animals, Gregor Lamb
Cat's Company, Ann Walker
Celebrating Nature, Gordon MacLellan
Celtic Faery Shamanism, Catrin James
Celtic Faery Shamanism - The Wisdom of the Otherworld, Catrin James
Celtic Lore & Druidic Ritual, Rhiannon Ryall
Celtic Sacrifice - Pre Christian Ritual & Religion, Marion Pearce
Celtic Saints and the Glastonbury Zodiac, Mary Caine
Circle and the Square, Jack Gale
Come Back To Life, Jenny Smedley
Company of Heaven, Jan McDonald
Compleat Vampyre - The Vampyre Shaman, Nigel Jackson
Cottage Witchcraft, Jan McDonald
Creating Form From the Mist - The Wisdom of Women in Celtic Myth and Culture, Lynne Sinclair-Wood
Crystal Clear - A Guide to Quartz Crystal, Jennifer Dent
Crystal Doorways, Simon & Sue Lilly

Crossing the Borderlines - Guising, Masking & Ritual Animal Disguise in the European Tradition, Nigel Pennick
Dragons of the West, Nigel Pennick
Dreamtime by Linda Louisa Dell
Dreamweaver by Elen Sentier
Earth Dance - A Year of Pagan Rituals, Jan Brodie
Earth Harmony - Places of Power, Holiness & Healing, Nigel Pennick
Earth Magic, Margaret McArthur
Egyptian Animals - Guardians & Gateways of the Gods, Akkadia Ford
Eildon Tree (The) Romany Language & Lore, Michael Hoadley
Enchanted Forest - The Magical Lore of Trees, Yvonne Aburrow
Eternal Priestess, Sage Weston
Eternally Yours Faithfully, Roy Radford & Evelyn Gregory
Everything You Always Wanted To Know About Your Body, But So Far Nobody's Been Able To Tell You, Chris Thomas & D Baker
Experiencing the Green Man, Rob Hardy & Teresa Moorey
Face of the Deep - Healing Body & Soul, Penny Allen
Fairies in the Irish Tradition, Molly Gowen
Familiars - Animal Powers of Britain, Anna Franklin
Flower Wisdom, Katherine Kear
Fool's First Steps, (The) Chris Thomas
Forest Paths - Tree Divination, Brian Harrison, Ill. S. Rouse
From Past to Future Life, Dr Roger Webber
From Stagecraft To Witchcraft, Patricia Crowther
Gardening For Wildlife Ron Wilson
God Year, The, Nigel Pennick & Helen Field
Goddess on the Cross, Dr George Young
Goddess Year, The, Nigel Pennick & Helen Field
Goddesses, Guardians & Groves, Jack Gale
Handbook For Pagan Healers, Liz Joan
Handbook of Fairies, Ronan Coghlan
Healing Book, The, Chris Thomas and Diane Baker
Healing Homes, Jennifer Dent
Healing Journeys, Paul Williamson
Healing Stones, Sue Philips
Heathen Paths - Viking and Anglo Saxon Beliefs by Pete Jennings
Herb Craft - Shamanic & Ritual Use of Herbs, Lavender & Franklin
Hidden Heritage - Exploring Ancient Essex, Terry Johnson
Hub of the Wheel, Skytoucher
In and Out the Windows, Dilys Gator
In Search of Herne the Hunter, Eric Fitch
In Search of the Green Man, Peter Hill
Inner Celtia, Alan Richardson & David Annwn
Inner Mysteries of the Goths, Nigel Pennick
Inner Space Workbook - Develop Through Tarot, Cat Summers & Julian Vayne
In Search of Pagan Gods, Teresa Moorey

Intuitive Journey, Ann Walker Isis - African Queen, Akkadia Ford
Journey Home, The, Chris Thomas
Kecks, Keddles & Kesh - Celtic Lang & The Cog Almanac, Bayley
Language of the Psycards, Berenice
Legend of Robin Hood, The, Richard Rutherford-Moore
Lid Off the Cauldron, Patricia Crowther
Light From the Shadows - Modern Traditional Witchcraft, Gwyn
Living Tarot, Ann Walker
Lore of the Sacred Horse, Marion Davies
Lost Lands & Sunken Cities (2nd ed.), Nigel Pennick
Lyblác, Anglo Saxon Witchcraft by Wulfeage
The Magic and Mystery of Trees, Teresa Moorey
Magic For the Next 1,000 Years, Jack Gale
Magic of Herbs - A Complete Home Herbal, Rhiannon Ryall
Magical Guardians - Exploring the Spirit and Nature of Trees, Philip Heselton
Magical History of the Horse, Janet Farrar & Virginia Russell
Magical Lore of Animals, Yvonne Aburrow
Magical Lore of Cats, Marion Davies
Magical Lore of Herbs, Marion Davies
The Magical Properties of Plants - and How to Find Them by Tylluan Penry
Magick Without Peers, Ariadne Rainbird & David Rankine
Masks of Misrule - Horned God & His Cult in Europe, Nigel Jackson
Medicine For The Coming Age, Lisa Sand MD
Medium Rare - Reminiscences of a Clairvoyant, Muriel Renard
Menopausal Woman on the Run, Jaki da Costa
Mind Massage - 60 Creative Visualisations, Marlene Maundrill
Mirrors of Magic - Evoking the Spirit of the Dewponds, P Heselton
The Moon and You, Teresa Moorey
Moon Mysteries, Jan Brodie
Mysteries of the Runes, Michael Howard
Mystic Life of Animals, Ann Walker
New Celtic Oracle The, Nigel Pennick & Nigel Jackson
Oracle of Geomancy, Nigel Pennick
Pagan Feasts - Seasonal Food for the 8 Festivals, Franklin & Phillips
Paganism For Teens, Jess Wynne
Patchwork of Magic - Living in a Pagan World, Julia Day
Pathworking - A Practical Book of Guided Meditations, Pete Jennings
Personal Power, Anna Franklin
Pickingill Papers - The Origins of Gardnerian Wicca, Bill Liddell
Pillars of Tubal Cain, Nigel Jackson
Places of Pilgrimage and Healing, Adrian Cooper
Planet Earth - The Universe's Experiment, Chris Thomas
Practical Divining, Richard Foord
Practical Meditation, Steve Hounsome
Practical Spirituality, Steve Hounsome
Psychic Self Defence - Real Solutions, Jan Brodie

Real Fairies, David Tame
Reality - How It Works & Why It Mostly Doesn't, Rik Dent
Romany Tapestry, Michael Houghton
Runic Astrology, Nigel Pennick
Sacred Animals, Gordon MacLellan
Sacred Celtic Animals, Marion Davies, Ill. Simon Rouse
Sacred Dorset - On the Path of the Dragon, Peter Knight
Sacred Grove - The Mysteries of the Forest, Yvonne Aburrow
Sacred Geometry, Nigel Pennick
Sacred Nature, Ancient Wisdom & Modern Meanings, A Cooper
Sacred Ring - Pagan Origins of British Folk Festivals, M. Howard
Season of Sorcery - On Becoming a Wisewoman, Poppy Palin
Seasonal Magic - Diary of a Village Witch, Paddy Slade
Secret Places of the Goddess, Philip Heselton
Secret Signs & Sigils, Nigel Pennick
The Secrets of East Anglian Magic, Nigel Pennick
A Seeker's Guide To Past Lives, Paul Williamson
Seeking Pagan Gods, Teresa Moorey
A Seer's Guide To Crystal Divination, Gale Halloran
Self Enlightenment, Mayan O'Brien
Soul Resurgence, Poppy Palin
Spirits of the Air, Jaq D Hawkins
Spirits of the Water, Jaq D Hawkins
Spirits of the Fire, Jaq D Hawkins
Spirits of the Aether, Jaq D Hawkins
Spirits of the Earth, Jaq D Hawkins
Stony Gaze, Investigating Celtic Heads John Billingsley
Stumbling Through the Undergrowth, Mark Kirwan-Heyhoe
Subterranean Kingdom, The, revised 2nd ed, Nigel Pennick
Symbols of Ancient Gods, Rhiannon Ryall
Talking to the Earth, Gordon MacLellan
Talking With Nature, Julie Hood
Taming the Wolf - Full Moon Meditations, Steve Hounsome
Teachings of the Wisewomen, Rhiannon Ryall
The Other Kingdoms Speak, Helena Hawley
Transformation of Housework, Ben Bushill
Treading the Mill - Practical CraftWorking in Modern Traditional Witchcraft by Nigel Pearson
Tree: Essence of Healing, Simon & Sue Lilly
Tree: Essence, Spirit & Teacher, Simon & Sue Lilly
Tree Seer, Simon & Sue Lilly
Torch and the Spear, Patrick Regan
Understanding Chaos Magic, Jaq D Hawkins
Understanding Second Sight, Dilys Gater
Understanding Spirit Guides, Dilys Gater
Understanding Star Children, Dilys Gater

The Urban Shaman, Dilys Gater
Vortex - The End of History, Mary Russell
Walking the Tides - Seasonal Rhythms and Traditional Lore in Natural Craft by Nigel Pearson
Warp and Weft - In Search of the I-Ching, William de Fancourt
Warriors at the Edge of Time, Jan Fry
Water Witches, Tony Steele
Way of the Magus, Michael Howard
Weaving a Web of Magic, Rhiannon Ryall
West Country Wicca, Rhiannon Ryall
What's Your Poison? vol 1, Tina Tarrant
Wheel of the Year, Teresa Moorey & Jane Brideson
Wildwitch - The Craft of the Natural Psychic, Poppy Palin
Wildwood King , Philip Kane
A Wisewoman's Book of Tea Leaf Reading, Pat Barki
The Witching Path, Moira Stirland
The Witch's Kitchen, Val Thomas
The Witches' Heart, Eileen Smith
Witches of Oz, Matthew & Julia Philips
Witchcraft Myth Magic Mystery and... Not Forgetting Fairies, Ralph Harvey
Wondrous Land - The Faery Faith of Ireland by Dr Kay Mullin
Working With Crystals, Shirley o'Donoghue
Working With Natural Energy, Shirley o'Donoghue
Working With the Merlin, Geoff Hughes
Your Talking Pet, Ann Walker
The Zodiac Experience, Patricia Crowther

FREE detailed catalogue
Contact: Capall Bann Publishing, Auton Farm, Milverton, Somerset, TA4 1NE
www.capallbann.co.uk